A Grace-Full Life

A Grace-Full Life
God's All-Reaching, Soul-Saving, Character-Shaping,
Never-Ending Love

A Grace-Full Life
978-1-5018-3281-9
978-1-5018-3282-6 *eBook*

A Grace-Full Life: Leader Guide
978-1-5018-3283-3
978-1-5018-3284-0 *eBook*

A Grace-Full Life: DVD
978-1-5018-3285-7

JORGE ACEVEDO & WES OLDS

A
GRACE-FULL
LIFE

§

GOD'S
ALL-REACHING,
SOUL-SAVING,
CHARACTER-SHAPING,
NEVER-ENDING
LOVE

Abingdon Press / Nashville

A GRACE-FULL LIFE
GOD'S ALL-REACHING, SOUL-SAVING,
CHARACTER-SHAPING, NEVER-ENDING LOVE

This book is printed on elemental chlorine-free paper.

Library of Congress Cataloging-in-Publication data applied for.

978-1-5018-3281-9

17 18 19 20 21 22 23 24 25 26 — 10 9 8 7 6 5 4 3 2 1
MANUFACTURED IN THE UNITED STATES OF AMERICA

We dedicate this book to our two mothers,
Carmen Acevedo and Sandy Olds,
who stand in the rich heritage of Mary,
the mother of Jesus. Like Mary, our mothers
have humbly lived as servants of the Lord
(Luke 1:38), faithfully treasured the promises of
God about us in their hearts (Luke 2:19),
presented us to the Lord as babies (Luke 2:22),
corrected us when we needed it (Luke 2:48),
and called out God's gifts in us (John 2:3-5).
You have modeled the grace-full life to us.

CONTENTS

ABOUT THE AUTHORS

Jorge Acevedo and **Wes Olds** are both pastors at Grace Church, a multi-site United Methodist congregation in southwest Florida with six campuses. The church has grown in its weekend attendance from 400 to over 2600 in the past nineteen years and has a remarkable ministry to, with, and for the poor, marginalized, and addicted. The church is recognized as having one of the largest and most effective recovery ministries in America.

Jorge is in his twenty-first year as the lead pastor at Grace Church and is the coauthor of *Sent: Giving the Gift of Hope at Christmas, Vital: Churches Changing Communities and the World* and *The Heart of Youth Ministry*. Born in Puerto Rico, Jorge moved with his family at age four months to the United States where he was raised. Jorge and his wife, Cheryl, are the parents of two sons and have four grandchildren. Jorge's passion is to connect people to God and the church.

Wes is in his eleventh year as the campus pastor of the Cape Coral campus of Grace Church and is also a leadership coach with Spiritual Leadership, Inc. (SLI). Wes and his wife, Becky, have one teenage son, Caleb. Wes's passions are helping people discover they are "Children of God and Persons of Worth" and serving as a change agent for local churches to return to biblical Christianity in the Wesleyan way.

Jorge and Wes have a unique thirty-three-year friendship that began when Jorge was Wes's youth pastor through his high school years. Together they have served at three churches for more than fifteen years.

In *A Grace-Full Life,* Jorge and Wes share a Wesleyan understanding of grace in a very warm, personal style with strong life application. Their approach is to speak in a unified voice (we) except when sharing their individual stories, which are identified by their names (in **bold** print within brackets). Their hope is that as you read, you will feel you are journeying together into a deeper understanding of God's amazing grace.

FOREWORD

Writer and Christian mystic Evelyn Underhill wrote that the interesting thing about religion is God.[1] I would take that insight a step further: the fascinating thing about God is grace. The grace of God, through the person of Jesus Christ and in the power of the Holy Spirit, is as mysterious and complex as human life itself. When we experience this grace, we blossom and flourish. Isolated from this grace, we hunger and thirst. Revivals and reformations have always been about access to the living stream of God's mercy, love, and grace. Sometimes this grace is hidden in plain sight. And at times our life stories, if we listen to them, are the unfolding of God's story in our own human experience.

Jorge Acevedo and Wes Olds are gifted evangelists, patient shepherds, transformational leaders, and wise teachers. They have listened to their lives—in the influence of mentors, relationships with their spouses, and the practice of ministry—and they have discovered the core (what John Wesley called the "marrow") of Christian teaching: the amazing grace of God that is, in their words, "even there, even now, even more, even when." They have not only listened; they have then taken the vulnerable step of bearing witness to the conversions and transformations in their lives. The strength of their witness is how this experience of grace among people is both different and similar.

The grace of God is radical, which is to say that it finds us where we are in our brokenness and failure. When leaders such as Jorge and Wes share the stories of their lives, they pierce the illusion of what success looks like. We may look at them—and the church they serve that reaches the unchurched, the working poor, and the addicted in profound and compelling ways—and our tendency might be to wonder, *how could this connect with my experience?* Yet it is the grace of God, the hunger for it (expressed in spiritual disciplines), and the trust that carries us through life, death, and life beyond death that is at the heart of these two leaders, their stories, and the story of Grace Church. Their transparency and honesty move us toward the same posture.

In listening to their voices and life stories, I was reminded of the adage that "what is most personal is most universal." Your journey may not look like theirs; but their willingness to submit to the "all-reaching, soul-saving, character-shaping, never-ending love" of God is a model of Wesleyan Christian witness. Along the way they have been disciples of Jesus Christ. Along the way they have been used by God to transform the world. How has this happened? They have been open to the possibility of a grace-full life.

In these pages you will discover not a program or a formula but a testimony of the messy, nonlinear, and unpredictable presence of a God who cares more about partnership than performance; more about engagement than ego. The interesting thing about religion is grace, and the compelling possibility for each of us as followers of Jesus is a grace-full life. It is the promise of the gospel grounded in the action of God with us and for us:

> *You are saved by God's grace because of your faith.*
> *This salvation is God's gift. It is not something you*
> *possessed. It's not something you did that you can be*

proud of. Instead, we are God's accomplishment, created in Christ Jesus to do good things. God planned for these good things to be the way we live our lives.

(Ephesians 2:8-10 CEB)

Bishop Ken Carter
Florida Conference, The United Methodist Church

Introduction

Most of us grew up hearing messages from our parents, teachers, and other leaders that sounded right to us then, but perhaps later in life we began to question them. How many of us heard messages like these?

> *Do your best!*
> *Keep your chin up!*
> *Work hard!*
> *There's no free lunch!*
> *If you want something done right, then do it yourself!*

Now, in and of themselves, these messages seem harmless and, frankly, can be helpful. There is nothing wrong with doing your best and working hard. We should. But there is a danger when these childhood messages creep into our relationship with God.

Here's the danger. These messages are all about our human efforts, abilities, and achievements. It's one thing if you apply this to playing Little League or practicing the piano. You might be the next Beethoven or Babe Ruth or Serena Williams, so do your best and work hard. But, sadly, when this message of effort, ability, and achievement creeps into our relationship with God, God becomes a cruel tyrant who wants us to do better, and we become beaten-down perfectionists who can never do enough, never measure up to please and appease our cruel, divine Taskmaster.

That's why we're so grateful for grace. Truth be told, we aren't just grateful for grace; we're counting on grace. Grace has been defined simply as God's unconditional love for all of creation. It's God's "crazy love"[1] for you. It's the reality that there is nothing you can do to make God love you more, and there's nothing you can do to make God love you less. Some anonymous wise person once gave the word *grace* this acrostic:

G *od's*
R *iches*
A *t*
C *hrist's*
E *xpenses*

Grace means that all our efforts, abilities, and achievements can never *make* God love and accept us, but in the gift of amazing grace through God's Son Jesus, "God demonstrates his own love for us…while we were still sinners" (Romans 5:8 NIV).

We like to think of it as a big umbrella with the word "GRACE" emblazoned on it. What we know of life from the womb to the

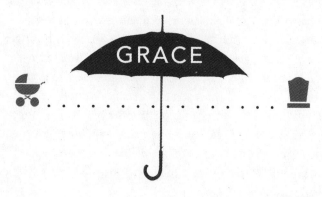

tomb is under grace whether we recognize it or not. Every human being that ever has been, is, or will be has lived under grace. Now, whether or not they live in and enjoy the benefits of grace is another discussion, but the Bible teaches clearly that God's grace is available to all.

The real question is: how do we experience grace in our journey from the womb to the tomb? Bible scholars and theologians have tried to describe the way we experience God's grace in different seasons of our lives. Some call it "the order of salvation" or *ordo salutus* in Latin. By reflecting on Holy Scripture, drawing upon our rich Christian tradition, using our God-given reason, and then rubbing it up against our experience in life, followers of Jesus in the Wesleyan stream identify four distinct seasons in which we experience God's grace in our life journey from the womb to the tomb.

The first season occurs before we become Christ-followers and is called *prevenient grace*. The God of creation and the universe, like an enamored lover, is wooing us into a relationship with God. The second season, *justifying* or *saving grace*, is the moment when we come to recognize and claim Jesus' saving work for ourselves. The third season is *sanctifying grace*, the journey to align our lives—in the power of the Holy Spirit and in the gift of Christian community—with the holiness of God. The fourth and final season of grace is *glorifying grace*; this is our journey from abundant life in this life to eternal life in the life to come. In the four chapters that follow, we will look to the Bible to get a better understanding and experience of this amazing grace of God. Here's the deal: the beauty of God's grace is that God desires for us to *live* in it! Grace transforms us, those around us, and our world.

There are four short phrases that describe these seasons of grace, all beginning with the word *even*:

- *Even there* God loves us. No matter where we go or what we do, God's grace is there. This is God's all-reaching, prevenient grace.
- *Even now* God loves us. God is in the rescuing business. This is God's soul-saving, justifying grace that is ours right now.
- *Even more* God loves us. Grace wants to grow us up into the likeness of Jesus. This is God's character-shaping, sanctifying grace.
- *Even when* God loves us. Grace carries us from this life to the next. This is God's never-ending, glorifying grace.

From the womb to the tomb, from the cradle to the grave, God loves us.

In 2013, Matt Redman, worship leader and contemporary Christian artist, released the song "Your Grace Finds Me." It masterfully and beautifully captures this womb-to-the-tomb, cradle-to-the-grave, first-to-last-breath grace of God in our lives. We love the way the song captures the breadth of God's amazing grace in our lives from our birth to our death. But the clarion call of the song is the simple affirmation of God's grace finding us:

Your grace finds me
Yes, Your grace finds me[2]

This is the journey of grace that every person on this blue-green planet called Earth is on, whether he or she recognizes it or not. God's grace finds us. Life is full of grace! Let's continue the journey together and dive deeper into God's amazing grace.

Jorge Acevedo and Wes Olds

CHAPTER 1

§

EVEN THERE
God's All-Reaching Love
(Prevenient Grace)

I can never escape from your Spirit!
I can never get away from your presence!
If I go up to heaven, you are there;
if I go down to the grave, you are there.
If I ride the wings of the morning,
if I dwell by the farthest oceans,
even there your hand will guide me,
and your strength will support me.

(Psalm 139:7-10)

We both are privileged to live and serve as pastors in Southwest Florida, one of the most beautiful places on the planet. Our community is situated at the mouth of the Caloosahatchee River as it dumps into the Gulf of Mexico. Spectacular, breathtaking beaches and prehistoric-looking manatees are the common stuff of our everyday lives. We often say, "Somebody has to suffer for Jesus and serve here, so it might as well be us!" We indeed are blessed to live and love in this part of God's creation.

[**Wes**] Several years ago, our family went out to eat at a local restaurant on the river. There was a long wait at the restaurant. Frankly, I was worn thin because of the normal challenges of ministry and life. So naturally, I was annoyed and suggested we go somewhere else. My family outvoted me, so we put our name on the wait list. Things suddenly changed, especially my cruddy attitude, when we decided to go outside and sit by the water as we waited for our name to be called. To our delight, we saw the most amazing sunset that captivated our attention, making the wait seem short.

As a majestic sky of blue, orange, and yellow exploded before us, reflecting onto the water, I sat in awe. After watching this breathtaking vista, we went in and had a delightful dinner. The scene, fresh seafood, and company soothed my weary soul. As we drove home, my son, Caleb, pulled my attention back to the expansive view for a second after-dinner sky show. "Look at that!" he said as he pointed up. In one part of the sky we could see planets shining brightly—Jupiter, Venus, and Mars. In another part we saw the moon and the Big Dipper. What a show! As I went to sleep that night, I had a renewed sense of wonder as I recognized again the ordinary beauty of God and his creation that surrounds me every day. I had been so busy that I really needed that time of star and soul gazing. I needed to slow down from the demands of daily life and simply look up.

In the Bible, David had a similar experience of awe and wonder while gazing at the night sky. We don't know what was going on that day when he stopped and looked up, but as he reflected on the experience, he wrote these words to God:

When I look at the night sky and see the work of your
fingers—
   the moon and the stars you set in place—
what are mere mortals that you should think about them,
   human beings that you should care for them?
                                             (Psalm 8:3-4)

David's stargazing caused him to soul-gaze and consider an amazing reality that many of us are either unaware of or too busy to ponder. The God who put the stars in outer space and put our sun and moon in place cares for you and me. We call God's constant love and care for us *grace*. Grace is the reality that the Creator of the universe deeply cares for and loves each and every one of us.

Jesus regularly taught about God's gracious love and care for every person on the planet. In the most famous message ever preached, the Sermon on the Mount, he was teaching wanna-be disciples then and now about the futility of chasing after money and the things money can buy.

After poignantly stating that you cannot serve both God and money, Jesus quickly reminds us why entrusting our lives to God is a very good thing:

> *"That is why I tell you not to worry about everyday*
> *life—whether you have enough food and drink, or*
> *enough clothes to wear. Isn't life more than food, and*
> *your body more than clothing? Look at the birds. They*
> *don't plant or harvest or store food in barns, for your*
> *heavenly Father feeds them. And aren't you far more*
> *valuable to him than they are? Can all your worries*
> *add a single moment to your life?*
>
> *"And why worry about your clothing? Look at the lilies*
> *of the field and how they grow. They don't work or*
> *make their clothing, yet Solomon in all his glory was*

not dressed as beautifully as they are. And if God cares
so wonderfully for wildflowers that are here today and
thrown into the fire tomorrow, he will certainly care for
you. Why do you have so little faith?"
(Matthew 6:25-30)

We have a God who is like a daddy anxious to care for the needs of his children. Jesus tells us to "look up" at the birds of the air and "look out" at the flowers of the fields. These are living witnesses to the gentle care and tender love of God. These are nature's testimonies of God's grace for you and me.

So right now, why don't you stop and take a moment to "look up" and "look out." Behold the light, majesty, and wonder of God's grace, which is more than we can comprehend. It is otherworldly, yet it surrounds us every day. Your life, your very breath is a gift of God's grace. God created the heavens and the earth, and God lovingly placed you in the midst of it all. The best description in the Bible of God's very essence and character is "God is love" (1 John 4:8), and God's love is unconditional.

[Jorge] I have a friend who, like me, is a grandfather. One of his grandkids was born prematurely and had to spend several weeks in the neonatal intensive care unit. They placed the baby in an incubator, and they put on rubber gloves and slipped their hands through the opening to hold the child. My friend told us that he wasn't satisfied holding his grandson with rubber gloves and looking at him through plastic. And then he spoke these words that I'll never forget: "I have discovered this about my grandson. He's crazy about me.... He just doesn't know it yet!"

That, my friends, is prevenient grace. That is God's "even there," all-reaching love. Every person on this planet is crazy about Jesus. They just don't know it yet. So, God is on an all-out search for us. This brings us to an important question.

In What Ways Is God an "Even There" God?

To answer this question, we want to look at one of David's amazing songs, Psalm 139. Packed in these twenty-four verses is an explosion of the character of our God who loved us long before we knew or acknowledged God's love for us. Psalm 139 tells us four things about the God who is drawing us into a relationship. Let's consider each one together.

1. God knows everything about each of us.

[Jorge] Cheryl and I have celebrated thirty-five years of marriage. We were married at ages eighteen and twenty-one. We became adults together, raised two sons together, finished three educational degrees together, bought three homes together, and have shared countless hours in genuine, deep, and honest conversation together.

[Wes] Becky and I have been married for twenty-four years, raised one son, finished four educational degrees, bought three homes, and also shared countless hours together in intimate conversation and memory making.

Here's the big question. Do our wives know everything about us? Well, the answer is an obvious "No!" Shucks, we don't even know everything about ourselves, but God does.

Look at how David, the shepherd, poet, and king, describes God's capacity to know everything about us:

> *O Lord, you have examined my heart*
> *and know everything about me.*
> *You know when I sit down or stand up.*
> *You know my thoughts even when I'm far away.*
> *You see me when I travel*
> *and when I rest at home.*
> *You know everything I do.*

You know what I am going to say
even before I say it, LORD.
(Psalm 139:1-4, emphasis added)

God has the capacity to look past the externals and into the core of who we really are. Theologians call this God's omniscience, which is God's capacity to know everything there is to know. Some might see this as frightening, but interestingly enough David saw it as comforting.

Both of us are ordained elders in The United Methodist Church. The process to be ordained as an elder in our church polity required that we intentionally engage in an extensive process of discernment. We had to discern whether we had the calling, gifts, and graces for ordained ministry, and so did the church. They "kicked the tires," and so did we.

The process involved many interviews by committees and boards, including thorough examinations of our physical, relational, psychological, financial, and theological wellness. It also involved years of mentoring, counseling, theological education, and field placement. Somewhere in the conference headquarters behind locked doors are two thick file folders with our names on them. These files are filled with "the good, the bad, and the ugly" of our lives. You could argue that those responsible for the process of ordination know more about us than we know about ourselves.

We both would testify that a candidate's attitude about the ordination process is the thing that makes or breaks it. If you are distrusting or defensive about the tedious requirements and the findings of the examinations, then not only will you find it very difficult but you also are less likely to be ordained. Yes, it is hard. Yes, the people involved do not always get it right. But if you distrust the process and the people leading the process, things will not go well. However, if you trust that the process and the people have good intentions, wanting the best interest for the church and for you, then all the information they have on you will not concern you.

The same thing is true about God's "file" on you. God knows everything about you—the good, the bad, and the ugly. God's omniscient knowledge of you can leave you feeling scared or secure. For David, God's knowledge about him brought security—despite all he went through as a follower of God with a huge assignment. How was that possible?

Remember that after David was anointed king, he served in the court of the reigning king, Saul, who was jealous of David's fame. Though David remained loyal, Saul's envy destroyed their relationship. Even after David ascended to the throne, his own son Absalom turned on him and ran David out of town. David had plenty of opportunities not to trust his all-knowing God.

Andy Stanley, lead pastor of North Point Ministries, has said that when there is an absence of information, we get to choose whether we will fill the gap with trust or suspicion.[1] For example, a colleague shows up late for an important meeting, and it creates this gap in your mind. "Is she late because she's a lazy, good-for-nothing worker?" is one gap-filler. Or, "Maybe she has a really good reason, and I'm waiting to hear what it is," is another gap-filling possibility. One is filled with suspicion while the other is filled with trust.

When it comes to our relationship with God, we do the same thing. In the absence of information, when life throws us a curveball, we get to choose. Will we fill the gap with suspicion or with trust? This is the challenge of every follower of Jesus.

[Jorge] For more than ten years, this gap has been a very real part of our family's experience. Our youngest son, Nathan, has wrestled with addiction and mental illness. This has led to arrests, jail time, overdoses, rehab, sleepless nights, and much more. At the same time, our ministry at Grace Church has expanded, as well as my responsibilities. Our church has grown from one campus to six and from a staff of five to a staff of more than one hundred. Particularly our ministry with the addicted, the poor, and those on the margin has garnered recognition within our denomination. Speaking engagements dot my schedule every month, and book projects have come my way. At church it has been remarkable, while at home it has been profoundly agonizing. Many times I have prayed to God, "Why, Lord? Why have you given us such a profound ministry around the world while our son at the end of the hallway suffers so badly?"

Yet Cheryl and I would testify that God is still good when life is hard. Throughout these horrendous days, it has been the knowledge that God has been working on our son's behalf even when Nathan has not known it that has brought us comfort. Most days by God's grace, we've been able to trust that our all-knowing God has our son and our lives in God's tender hands. We have chosen to fill the gap with trust.

2. God is everywhere we go.

In addition to a shared vocation and many other things that we have in common, we both are always on the hunt for a deal. Recently we found an app for our cell phones that can tell us about deals in stores as we drive or walk by them. Everywhere we go, our phones know where we are, and this app hunts down a deal. God is like that, too. God knows everywhere we go and wants to give us the deal of a lifetime. God wants to shower us with undeserved grace.

Over the years, we have heard a number of testimonies in which people have said, "I tried to run from God, but no matter where I went, God would find me." Here's how David describes this sentiment in Psalm 139:

You go before me and follow me.
> *You place your hand of blessing on my head.*
Such knowledge is too wonderful for me,
> *too great for me to understand!*

I can never escape from your Spirit!
> *I can never get away from your presence!*
If I go up to heaven, you are there;
> *if I go down to the grave, you are there.*
If I ride the wings of the morning,
> *if I dwell by the farthest oceans,*
even there your hand will guide me,
> *and your strength will support me.*
I could ask the darkness to hide me
> *and the light around me to become night—*
> *but even in darkness I cannot hide from you.*
To you the night shines as bright as day.
> *Darkness and light are the same to you.*
> > *(vv. 5-12)*

David declares that neither the heights of heaven nor the depths of hell are beyond God's reach. God echoes the prophet Isaiah, who said, "Surely the arm of the LORD is not too short to save" (Isaiah 59:1a NIV). Theologians call this God's omnipresence, which is God's capacity to be everywhere.

Every Sunday we have a team that goes into the juvenile detention center to share God's love and grace with the adolescent boys who are incarcerated there. Recently one of the team members we'll call Eric told us about a conversation he had with a teen we'll call Andrew. As Andrew opened up and began sharing his story with Eric, he said that he had been running with the wrong crowd and had broken into cars in our community. One day he got caught, and the judge sent him to the detention center.

Eric listened and then shared that he had been the victim of a similar crime, telling how it had shaken up both him and his family. He described hearing a noise in his driveway, running out to confront the robbers, and then calling the police. As he recounted the details, Andrew became strangely quiet and increasingly uncomfortable. Their time together ended, and Eric went home.

The next Sunday when Eric arrived at the detention center, Andrew invited him to sit with him on the couch for a private discussion. There Andrew confessed that he remembered Eric— that he had been the one who had robbed him. Eric, his new spiritual mentor, forgave him and promised to be his advisor and help him as he seeks to change his life. Then Eric shared with Andrew about Jesus and God's love.

Now, we don't believe for a second that God caused Andrew to steal. But God was at work in that darkness. You could say it is a coincidence that a boy broke into a car a year ago and then months later...

- a guy heard about a new ministry opportunity to serve youth in a detention center,
- the Holy Spirit tapped him on the shoulder to join the ministry team,
- he signed up, went to training, and was cleared to be a mentor,
- that guy randomly was assigned to the same kid who robbed him,
- and after making that discovery through the kid's own confession, he was able to offer forgiveness.

That may be what some people call a coincidence, but we call it prevenient grace. You may try to outrun the law, but you cannot outrun God's love.

God is persistent, tireless, and lovingly resolved to convince us to recognize and respond to his grace. God makes the Energizer Bunny look lazy! God's love keeps on going and going and going.

Francis Thomson was an opium-addicted seminary dropout who discovered God's pursuit of him and wrote a poem in which he called God "The Hound of Heaven" because of God's relentless love. Like a hound dog catches a scent and recklessly pursues it, God has caught your scent and will not relent until you are caught by his grace. In the classic devotional *My Utmost for His Highest*, Oswald Chambers wrote, "Sometimes...[I] wish [God] would leave me alone, and He does not."[2] God's relentless tenderness works to awaken our souls to his invitation to come live in "the unforced rhythms of grace" (Matthew 11:28-30 *The Message*).

3. God made each one of us.

A member of our recovery group was sharing his testimony years ago, and he told of God's relentless, all-out search for him when he was lost in addiction and the insane behavior that accompanied it. Then he said these words we'll never forget: "The God I didn't believe in, believed in me." Why? Because God made him, just as God made you, me, and every other person on this planet.

The psalmist David describes it this way in Psalm 139:

> *You made all the delicate, inner parts of my body*
> *and knit me together in my mother's womb.*
> *Thank you for making me so wonderfully complex!*
> *Your workmanship is marvelous—how well I know it.*
> *You watched me as I was being formed in utter seclusion,*
> *as I was woven together in the dark of the womb.*

You saw me before I was born.
Every day of my life was recorded in your book.
Every moment was laid out
before a single day had passed.

How precious are your thoughts about me, O God.
They cannot be numbered!
I can't even count them;
they outnumber the grains of sand!
And when I wake up,
you are still with me!

(vv. 13-18)

Like a master craftsman, God shaped, formed, and fashioned every one of us. As the Apostle Paul wrote, "For we are his workmanship" (Ephesians 2:10a KJV). God made you, and that's why he's on an all-out search for you!

[Jorge] When my boys were young, they would make drawings in school and at church, and like good parents we would display them on the refrigerator. After several weeks, the drawings would be tattered and torn—even food stained. Late at night when the boys were asleep, we would take the drawings off the refrigerator and throw them away. More than once, our boys busted us. They would find their drawings in the trash can and say, with tears streaming down their pudgy little faces, "Mommy, Daddy, why did you throw away our masterpiece?" Friend, whether you know it or not, you are God's masterpiece. God made you with amazing possibilities and tremendous potential. Sin wants to throw you in the trash can, but grace wants to rescue you.

[Wes] My son, Caleb, is in high school. I've not done everything right as a dad, but I've tried to pray for my son regularly. A few months ago, I read a verse in the Bible that I sensed God nudging me to pray for Caleb. So, for many days and even sometimes at family dinner, I would pray Ephesians 2:10, which says, "We are God's masterpiece. He has created us anew in Christ Jesus, so we can do the good things he planned for us long ago."

One night Caleb went to our church's senior high youth meeting, and a young woman was there to share her testimony and life verse. She had some printed Scripture verses for the kids to come forward and pick up. Caleb was last in line, and the verse he got was Ephesians 2:10! The next week, the youth message was built on—guess what verse—Ephesians 2:10! Sometime later, the young people were given bars of soap with scriptures written on them, symbolizing that God cleanses their souls. When Caleb grabbed a bar of soap, guess what verse was written on it? Ephesians 2:10! One night I said to my son, "I think God wants you to know that you '*are God's masterpiece . . . created . . . in Christ Jesus. . . .*'"

As I went over this story with Caleb in preparation for sharing it here, he commented that the verse is not about one person but all of us: "We are God's masterpiece. . ." Friend, whether you know it or not, *you* are God's masterpiece. God made you with amazing possibilities and tremendous potential.

4. God can handle our "ugly."

When we read Psalm 139, the first eighteen verses are pure poetry. David elegantly describes God in amazing terms. Some of the most robust and thoughtful words ever written about God are found here. Then we get to verse 19, and David slams on the brakes and does a one-hundred-eighty-degree turn in tone and content. Look at the dramatic shift:

> *O God, if only you would destroy the wicked!*
> *Get out of my life, you murderers!*
> *They blaspheme you;*
> *your enemies misuse your name.*

O Lord, shouldn't I hate those who hate you?
Shouldn't I despise those who oppose you?
Yes, I hate them with total hatred,
for your enemies are my enemies.

(vv. 19-22)

Wow! That's some change in perspective! From the rapturous virtues of God who knows everything, is everywhere, and made everything to "God, kill my enemies!" But let's be real here, friend. Isn't life an odd mix of reverence and revenge? Life is a contact sport, and as we journey with Jesus, people hurt us and we hurt ourselves. We love that David doesn't whitewash the pain and sorrow of life or the residual bitterness, resentment, and rage it can create in us.

God is not afraid of your "ugly."
In the middle of the raw stuff of
your life, God pursues you.

Here's the deal: God is not afraid of your "ugly." In the middle of the raw stuff of your life, God pursues you. The story of the Bible is God's gigantic search-and-rescue mission for humanity. When Adam and Eve hid in the garden of Eden, God came searching for them in the cool of the day. When Moses escaped to Midian, God found him at the burning bush. When Elijah hid in a cave, God showed up for a visit. When Peter hovered around the fire after denying he knew Jesus three times, Jesus caught his eye. You see, as the popular song says, "there ain't no mountain high enough, ain't no valley low enough"[3]—and we would add, praise God, that there ain't no trouble or sin deep enough—to separate you from the love of God that is yours in Christ! Romans 8:39 puts it this way: "Nothing in all creation will ever be able to separate us from the love of God that is revealed in Christ Jesus our Lord."

It is important to note that David, who penned Psalm 139, was the second king of Israel. Do you remember the story? Saul, the first king of Israel, began his reign with such promise. He literally stood head and shoulders above all the other young men in the tribe of Benjamin, and his dad was rich and famous. So with Saul's good looks and impressive stature and wealth, it was little surprise that the prophet Samuel choose him to be the first king of the new nation of Israel.

Saul began his reign well and with humility. But the heavy responsibilities of leading the nation plus his own predisposition to rely on himself became his downfall. So Samuel was charged by God to find a new king. His dilemma was that Saul was still king. Frankly, Samuel was worried that Saul would have him killed if he caught wind of his God-given assignment. So Samuel did what any prophet worth his weight in salt would do; he consulted God. God told him to go to a small town near Jerusalem named Bethlehem, and there he would find a man named Jesse who had a whole bunch of boys—one of whom God had chosen to succeed the wayward Saul.

When Samuel arrived at Jesse's home, he saw his oldest son, Eliab, and he said to himself, "This has got to be the one!" It seems that, just like Saul, Eliab was quite the specimen of manhood; but God interrupted Samuel's speculation and gave him a paradigm shift, saying:

> *"Don't judge by his appearance or height, for I have rejected him. The LORD doesn't see things the way you*

see them. People judge by outward appearance, but the
LORD looks at the heart."

(1 Samuel 16:7)

God reoriented Samuel's evaluation process, explaining that it wasn't about appearance or stature but the heart. You see, God's measuring stick is different than ours. We humans tend to rely on good looks, chiseled physiques, educational horsepower, or economic potency; but not God. God's ways are not our ways (see Isaiah 55:8).

So, one by one, Jesse paraded seven of his sons in front of the man of God, and one by one, God whispered in Samuel's ear, "Nope. Not this one." Samuel asked Jesse, "Do you have any more sons?"

"Well, there is the youngest, but he's out back tending sheep," Jesse answered.

"Bring him to me," Samuel commanded. David was his name, and indeed he was the one chosen by God to be the next king of Israel. God told Samuel, "This is the one I have chosen." I'd imagine Jesse and his seven other sons' jaws dropped.

There are two things we want you to notice about this powerful story. First, David was not numbered. When his father was asked by Samuel to bring his sons, he presented seven to Samuel. Samuel had to ask, "Are there any others?" Then and only then did Jesse basically say, "Well, yeah, there is one more." He didn't have seven sons. He had eight. Can you imagine what not being counted by his own father did to David's soul? "You don't count!" must have echoed over and over again in the shepherd boy's heart.

Second, David was not named. When Samuel asked if Jesse had any more sons, he called David "the youngest." There was no term of endearment here. Jesse wasn't a proud father who puffed out his chest and introduced his youngest son. Instead, he called him by the Hebrew word *qaton*, which most translations render as "the youngest." However, the word has much deeper significance, because literally it means "insignificant." David's own father not only did not number him but also did not name him, instead calling him insignificant—unimportant, irrelevant, and inconsequential.

We've lived life long enough to know that all God's children and all God's families are dysfunctional. It's part of the sin problem on this planet evident in our nations, communities, families, workplaces, and schools—and in each of us individually. Even the best parents doing their best parenting leave their children with some kind of "hole in their soul." Each of us knows to some degree or another David's sense of being unnamed and unnumbered. But is this "hole in our soul" fatal and final? Not to our God "who is able, through his mighty power at work within us, to accomplish infinitely more than we might ask or think" (Ephesians 3:20). Let's go back to the story.

What happened next was the game changer for the unnumbered, insignificant sheepherder:

> So as David stood there among his brothers, Samuel took the flask of olive oil he had brought and anointed David with the oil. And the Spirit of the LORD came powerfully upon David from that day on. Then Samuel returned to Ramah.
>
> *(1 Samuel 16:13)*

This is the first time in this story that David is named. Until this moment when he is anointed with oil and the Holy Spirit, David's identity was "unnumbered" and "unnamed." From this moment on, David was filled with the Holy Spirit, and ultimately he used his God-given gifts to establish Israel as a great nation.

Here's the deal, friend. In one way or another, we all know what it is like to feel unnumbered and unnamed. This is part of the "ugly" of our lives. But this is not the truth about you, just as it was not the truth about David. God saw gifts in David, and God sees gifts in you—even if you feel unnumbered and unnamed. Our "ugly" does not disqualify us from God's grace.

David had experienced God as the one who knew everything about him and everywhere he went and who had made David a masterpiece. Years later as king, David committed adultery and murder, to name just a few of his sins, and he again discovered the God who could handle his "ugly." And God can handle your "ugly," too!

But Psalm 139 doesn't end there. After declaring the majesty of God in the first eighteen verses and then honestly showing God his "ugly" in the next four verses, David ends with an amazing prayer:

> *Search me, O God, and know my heart;*
> *test me and know my anxious thoughts.*
> *Point out anything in me that offends you,*
> *and lead me along the path of everlasting life.*
> *(vv. 23-24)*

David invites the God who has been on an all-out pursuit of his life to look deep within him and point out anything that separates him from God. David uses verbs such as *search*, *test*, and *point out* in his prayer. He's asking God to do a heart catheterization on him.

David trusts the God who knows everything about him, the God who knows everywhere he goes, the God who made him, and, yes, even the God who can handle his "ugly." We're pretty confident that God had a talk with David about his anger problem with his enemies, too. David teaches us that God is an "even there" God.

"Asta Aye!"

Several years ago, we were invited to Costa Rica to teach several dozen local pastors at their seminary. One morning we were teaching on the subject of God's "even there" prevenient grace, and we told story after story of people at our church whom Jesus had found in places such as strip clubs and bars. We did our dead-level best to convince them of God's activity "even there." In Spanish, the word for "even there" is "*asta aye*." Over and over again, we would say, "*El Señor está asta aye*"—"The Lord is even there." The pastors were not convinced and kept saying back to us, "*No. El Señor no está asta aye*," which means, "No, the Lord is not even there." You see, their theology taught them that God could never be in hellish places such as strip clubs and bars. God was too holy for that.

In the back of the room, a guy who didn't look like the others stood up and asked for permission to speak. He was wearing a Harley Davidson T-shirt, leather jacket, and jeans and was covered with tattoos. The rest of the crowd was dressed— well, can we just say "more proper." He then told about walking out of a bar one night in Mexico and encountering a bunch of Christians who started to witness to him about God's love. They gave him a tract, a little pamphlet that explained how to start a relationship with God, and he shoved it in his backpack, pushed the crowd aside, jumped on his Harley, and left.

Months later, this same man was at the end of his rope. Filled with despair and darkness, he sat at a bar in Costa Rica to drink his last drink of rum. After walking upstairs to his room above the bar and sitting on his bed, he reached in his backpack to grab his gun and kill himself, but instead he pulled out the tract. He began to read the little pamphlet about a God who loved him right where he was and who sent Jesus, God's own Son, to die on the cross so that his sins could be forgiven. Tears streamed down his face as that hardened biker became a follower of Jesus.

At this point the man said to the pastors in training at the seminary, "¡*El Señor está asta aye!*"—"The Lord is even there!" With that, the room exploded in praise and adoration of the God of whom Isaiah said, "Surely the arm of the LORD is not too short to save" (Isaiah 59:1 NIV).

Our God is an "even there" God who is able to reach us no matter how far we have drifted away. This may be a word from God for someone you profoundly love who is on the run from God. Rest assured, God is there and actively working to woo your loved one to himself. Or perhaps this word from God is for you. Like the prodigal son on the run from his father's love and protection, you may wonder if you have journeyed too far from the Father's reach. Let us assure you that you have not. The God of the universe is at work. God loves you and wants you to come home.

CHAPTER 2

§

EVEN NOW
God's Soul-Saving Love

(Justifying Grace)

*As God's partners, we beg you not to accept this
marvelous gift of God's kindness and then ignore it.
For God says,*

> *"At just the right time, I heard you.
> On the day of salvation, I helped you."*

*Indeed, the "right time" is now. Today is the day of
salvation.*

(2 Corinthians 6:1-2)

[Wes] I remember the first time that I saw my wife, Becky. She
was on the University of Kentucky marching band field—a dancer
with blonde hair. She was a freshman, and I was a junior. I watched
her the entire practice; her every move captivated my attention. To
my delight, she showed up about a week later at a Bible study that
met on our college campus. I honestly cannot tell you anything

that study was about, but I remember every move she made. I remember watching her laugh with her friends and cry as she was touched by God's Word. She was beautiful inside and out.

I do remember making one decision that night: to get to know her and her friends so that I could soon ask her out on a date! I worked hard at this, and on one great night I got up the nerve after the Bible study to walk across the room and ask her out. To my surprise, she said, "Yes!" Then I realized I had a problem. I didn't have any nice clothes to take her out to a respectable place. I panicked and picked up the phone to call the only person I knew who could help. I said, "Mom, you can never tell anyone this, but you've got to take me shopping!"

With me wearing a new outfit, Becky and I went on our first date. At the end of the night, I summoned all my courage and asked if she would like to go out again. She said, "Yes!" again. The next day, I picked up the phone and called my mom again. Time for more shopping!

This drama went on for months. Finally, at month eleven, I was ready to make a full-on commitment to Becky. I had earned extra money and bought a small ring. I secretly scheduled a meeting with her parents to ask permission to marry their daughter. It was graciously granted. I took her on a date—dressed in more new clothes—nervously sang a song to her while playing my guitar, and gave her roses. After the song, I got down on one knee and asked the question: "Becky, will you marry me?" And she said, "Yes!" one more time.

Here's the deal, though. Becky had no idea of all that went on behind the scenes in order for me to finally hear her "yes." She didn't know the agonizing nights of prayer and planning. She didn't know about me shopping with my mom, earning extra money to pay for the ring, or having a secret meeting with her parents. All of those efforts were done just hear her say "Yes" to my proposal.

The Bible often is described as a dynamic love story. In the New Testament, Jesus compares himself to a bridegroom longing to be with his bride. If the seasons of grace were to be compared to a couple's relationship, God's prevenient, "even there" grace would be the season of dating. It's the work God does before we say "yes" to God. God's soul-saving, justifying, "even now" grace makes us able to respond to God's proposal for a relationship that He has been pursuing with us since before we were even aware of it—all to hear us say "yes" to God's proposal of grace.

Light Switch or Dimmer Switch?

Our personal as well as pastoral experience is that this "yes" can come in a moment or in a season of a person's life. Some people become followers of Jesus in what we call a "light switch" experience. Think of the Apostle Paul's conversion on the Damascus Road (Acts 9). One moment the person is not a follower of Jesus. Then in an instant, like a light switch being flipped on, the Holy Spirit reaches them and they say "yes" to Jesus.

[Jorge] That was my experience. I was raised in what I would call a nominally church-going home. My mom had a heart for God and attended worship services regularly. I had a "drug" problem; my mother "drug" me to church. The last time I recall being in church as a boy was when I was about thirteen. My neighborhood buddy, Alex, and I were acting like testosterone-filled, trouble-seeking adolescents and got called down by the pastor. Embarrassed, I left church that night and didn't return for five years.

In that half-decade, I traveled down the roads of drugs, alcohol, and sexual promiscuity. Like all teenagers, my need to be needed was raging, coupled with my disdain for any parental or educational authority in my life. Ironically, I was a very good student. Because my mother was an educator and maintaining good grades was a high value in our home, I did that—but frankly, it was only to keep my parents off my back. Those good grades became the disguise behind which I hid my unhealthy and unholy behavior. A major knee surgery following a football injury at the age of fifteen robbed me of my identity as a "jock" on my high school campus, throwing me further into my quest for identity—which led to more drugs and alcohol.

During my senior year in high school, John Zilen, the area director for a campus ministry, brought his ministry team to our school. Their strategy was to find the leaders of the school and build relationships with them. John and his team knew that if they could win a leader to Christ, then that student leader could influence his or her friends for Christ. For some reason (I now know it was God's wooing, "even there" grace), I was asked by John to join a small group with several of my high school friends. I said "yes." We studied a little workbook that dealt with topics such as who is God, who is Jesus, and what is the Bible.

One night the group was meeting in my home. That night John said to us, "God can change your life," and something inside me stirred. I asked what might have been the first serious question of my young life. "John, what difference can God make in my life?" I cannot recall all of what John said, but something deep within resonated with what John was saying. He told my friends and me that Jesus could give us a reason and purpose for our lives. At that time in my life, I had no plans for my future except the next high and the next girl. So that night I bowed my head and did what Sam Shoemaker said everyone can do. I gave as much of myself as I could to as much of God as I understood.[1] I surrendered my life to Jesus. This was the single most defining moment of my life, and it happened in an instant. It was like I drove a stake in ground and tethered myself to it. Everything would be different after that single moment. It was my "light switch" salvation experience.

Others become followers of Jesus in a "dimmer switch" experience. A dimmer switch allows you to slowly increase the brightness of a light. When you click the knob on, the light is very dim. Then, as you turn the knob, the light shines brighter and brighter. A biblical example of a dimmer switch experience of grace is the bewildered disciples on the Emmaus Road who met the stranger, Jesus, as they walked with him. Confused because of Jesus' death on the cross, they wondered what their future held. Their witness was, "Didn't our hearts burn within us as he talked with us on the road?" (Luke 24:32). In the journey of walking and talking with Jesus, their hearts were warmed. It wasn't a moment. It was more like a season.

[**Wes**] My own salvation experience was like a dimmer switch. My "yes" to God came over several seasons in my childhood and adolescence. My parents had me baptized as an infant, promising God and the church...

- "to live before [Wes] a life that becomes the Gospel; to exercise all godly care that he be brought up in the Christian faith, that he be taught the Holy Scriptures, and that he learn to give reverent attendance upon the private and public worship of God."
- "to keep [Wes] under the ministry and guidance of the church until he by the power of God shall accept for himself the gift of salvation, and be confirmed as a full and responsible member of Christ's holy Church."[2]

They lived into these vows, claiming God's prevenient grace in my life.

When I was five, my mom was watching a Billy Graham television special while I was in the room. She says that when he gave the altar invitation to a stadium full of people, I dropped my toys and prayed the prayer with him. When I was twelve, I said "yes" to God's love as I made my first public profession of faith in Jesus at my confirmation. When I was sixteen, Jorge took our youth group to work with the poor in the inner city, and I felt the light of Jesus grow brighter in me. Once again I said "yes" to living my life as a follower of his. This has been my "dimmer switch" experience of God's "even now," justifying grace.

So one of us responded to God's justifying grace in a "light switch" moment while the other responded in a "dimmer switch" season.

In our unscientific surveys as we talk with people about their experience of saying "yes" to Jesus, about 80 percent describe a "dimmer switch" season while about 20 percent say they have had a "light switch" moment. Here's the deal: It doesn't matter how and when we respond to God's proposal of grace in our lives. What matters is that we respond! Right now God is extending a hand of relationship in hopes that we would simply say "yes" to God's love in this moment or season of life.

As we consider God's "even now" grace that saves and justifies, remember that God longs to be in a continually growing relationship with you. Long before you are aware of God's grace, God looks forward to the day or season in your life when you will say "yes" to this proposal. God's saving grace is available "even now." In 2 Corinthians 6:2 we read, "For God says, 'At just the right time, I heard you. On the day of salvation, I helped you.' Indeed, the 'right time' is *now*. Today is the day of salvation" (*emphasis added*).

This is good news, but only if we realize that we need saving.

The Goodness Ladder

There have been times when we both have started to subtly believe and live a lie that says we can "get our salvation" the old-fashioned way—by earning it! Many people trust in a "performance

46

plan" approach to finding salvation and lasting peace. We cannot tell you how many times we have talked with others about their relationship with God, and the first words out of their mouths go something like this: "Well, I try to be a good person…" Now, that's a good thing. But when we are talking about having a relationship with a holy, perfect God, our "goodness" does not and cannot make up the gap.

One of our favorite preachers and leaders is Bill Hybels, senior pastor of Willow Creek Community Church. He once shared a powerful illustration in a message to visualize the way we human beings tend to grade ourselves on a "goodness scale,"[3] by saying, "I'm worse than so and so" or "I'm better than such and such." As we compare ourselves to others in this way, we are essentially attempting to climb the ladder and earn our salvation.

Imagine, if you will, a huge ladder representing a scale of goodness from absolutely, perfectly good (at the top) to absolutely, utterly evil (at the bottom). Of course, *God* is at the top of this ladder as the only One who is perfectly good. Now here's the question to consider: Where do you and I fit on this goodness ladder? When it comes to our goodness—our capacity to live a Christ-honoring life—where are we on the scale from absolute goodness to utter wickedness?

To help us get some perspective about where we think we might fit on this ladder of goodness, consider where we might place a few other people on the ladder. The first name is Mother Teresa. Remember that she was the Albanian founder of the Missionaries of Charity, an organization committed to the poorest of the poor on our planet. Though now deceased, her ministry has over 5,000 sisters working in over 130 countries doing acts of kindness for forgotten and thrown-away people.[4] She was probably one of the most kind, benevolent, and caring human beings ever, but was she perfectly good? We read excerpts from her journals and see that

Mother Teresa struggled with doubts and fears just as all of us do, so she's not perfectly good—though she might be really high on the ladder. We might choose to place Mother Teresa near the top of the ladder.

Now think of John Wesley, who led untold numbers of people to faith in Christ and began a religious movement in England that spread internationally, leading to the founding of Methodism. But was John Wesley perfectly good? Though he believed in Christian perfection or sanctification, he acknowledged that this did not mean we are entirely free from sin. He admitted that he himself fell short of perfection and was being made into the image of Christ. We might put John Wesley just a little above or below Mother Teresa, depending on our perspective.

Here's the question again for those of us living on the "performance plan" when it comes to our relationship with God: *Where do you and I fit on this goodness ladder?* Do we think we are 60 percent good? Fifty percent good? Forty percent good? If we're honest, most of us probably would say that we fall somewhere below Mother Teresa and John Wesley.

This simple ladder exercise accentuates the fallacy of trying to "be good" before a holy God. When it comes to the issue of goodness, we all fall short. Paul had it right when he said, "For everyone has sinned; we all fall short of God's glorious standard" (Romans 3:23). That's why we are not just grateful for grace; we are counting on grace!

You see, instead of us trying to climb some "goodness ladder" to be in a relationship with God, here's what God does. You may have heard that "God so loved the world that he gave his only Son..." (John 3:16 NRSV). Here's what that means. God sent Jesus down from heaven, down "the ladder," to meet us just as we are. The story of Jesus is one of downward mobility. But the good news of Jesus is that we don't have to climb our way into heaven. Heaven has come to us. God is a missionary God who is on an all-out search-and-rescue mission for all people everywhere and in every time who are made in God's image.

This rescue mission is evident in Jesus' earthly ministry. In the Gospel of Luke there is the story of a man who spent his life climbing and striving until he discovered Jesus' salvation. The story begins in Luke 19:1-3:

> *Jesus entered Jericho and made his way through the town. There was a man there named Zacchaeus. He was the chief tax collector in the region, and he had become very rich. He tried to get a look at Jesus, but he was too short to see over the crowd.*

Often in the four Gospels, tax collectors are lumped in with "other notorious sinners." These Jewish men were despised not only by the Romans, who used them to extort as much money as possible from their own Jewish kindred, but also by the Jews whom they extorted. Their only friends were other tax collectors.

Somehow Zacchaeus, a very wealthy man, got the news that Jesus was passing through his town of Jericho, and something about Jesus drew Zacchaeus to him. He didn't know it, but it was God's prevenient, "even there" grace at work. There was what N. T. Wright calls the "echoes of a voice"[5] that drew him to want to be in a relationship with Jesus. Zacchaeus had spent his life climbing the ladder of success and found it was leaning against the wrong wall. He longed for a savior. What he discovered can help all of us answer a critical question.

Why Does God Want to Have a Personal Relationship with Me?

Luke is a masterful writer, and he includes in his description of Zacchaeus that he was short. But Zacchaeus wasn't short in stature only. He was short on the experience of grace that Jesus wanted to offer him—and that Jesus offers each of us, too. So Zacchaeus went out on a limb to see—and to find—the Savior he needed.

In this story, we see three things that God wants to give us through his justifying grace—his *charis,* which means "that which affords joy, pleasure, delight, sweetness, charm, loveliness."[6] Let's consider each of these gifts of justifying grace.

1. God wants to give us friendship.

We read an article in the *New York Times* on adult friendships in which the author gives three reasons friendships are important. First, "friendship helps people make better judgments." Together friends can think through problems and situations. Second, "friends usually bring out better versions of each other." Around a good friend, the best "you" comes out. Finally, "people behave better if they know their friends are observing."[7] People tend to want to live up to their friends' high regard.

Friendships are important, and Zacchaeus needed a friend who could do all three of these things in his life. Remember, Zacchaeus would have been a hated, despised man. I'm sure when he walked by others, he was called a lot of names. He had earned the title "chief" in the tax collecting business, yet not even that title could satisfy. I get the sense that he was a lonely guy. When Jesus saw him, he was alone atop a tree—a fitting picture of his life of climbing. Look at what happened next:

> So he ran ahead and climbed a sycamore-fig tree beside the road, for Jesus was going to pass that way.
>
> When Jesus came by, he looked up at Zacchaeus and called him by name. "Zacchaeus!" he said. "Quick, come down! I must be a guest in your home today."
>
> (Luke 19:4-5)

Two powerful , grace-filled things happen in these verses. First of all, Jesus called Zacchaeus by name. We don't know how Jesus knew his name; maybe he was so "notorious" that Jesus had heard about him. We don't know. But we know that Jesus called him Zacchaeus. Maybe it had been a long time since someone had called him by name.

A group of children were asked, "How do you know what love is?" Here are some of their responses:

> *"Love is when you go out to eat and give somebody most of your french fries without making them give you any of theirs." (Danny, age 7)*

> *"When my grandmother got arthritis, she couldn't bend over and paint her toenails anymore. So my grandfather does it for her all the time, even when his hands got arthritis too. That's love." (Brenda, age 8)*

> *"When someone loves you, the way they say your name is different. You know that your name is safe on their lips." (Billy, age 5)*

We think Billy was on to something. That's the way we imagine this scene. The way Jesus said "Zacchaeus" was different; his name was safe on Jesus' lips. Jesus knew his name and called to him.

Tommy Walker, a prolific worship leader and songwriter, wrote the song "He Knows My Name" at the request of his pastor who was preaching on John 10:3, which says, "He calls his own sheep by name." Sometime later Tommy met a boy named Jerry in an orphanage in the Philippines. Every day Jerry would ask, "Tommy, what's my name?" and Tommy would answer, telling him that someone much greater knew his name. Jerry was an orphan who had a deep desire to be known. And Tommy was able to sing "He Knows My Name" to Jerry and many of his orphan friends.[8]

It's not only the Jerrys of this world who desire to be known. It's all of us. All of us want to hear Jesus call our name.

Another grace-filled event happened for Zacchaeus when Jesus said to him, "I must be a guest in your home today." Sharing a meal together was a big deal in that time and culture. To recline at a table with others was a sacred sign of acceptance and love. Who knows how long it had been since Zacchaeus had had someone over for dinner. So Jesus said to this guy alone in a tree, "Come down." Zacchaeus had been short on friends until Jesus befriended him. Of all the homes in town, Jesus was coming to Zacchaeus's home!

Jesus was essentially saying, "Stop your climbing, Zacchaeus. Come down from your attempts to earn my love by being good enough. Accept my love for you. I want to be your friend." Zacchaeus was about to experience the truth of the famous words written by Joseph Scriven: "What a friend we have in Jesus."[9] We are thankful that the children's ministry teams at our church are faithful in extending God's offer of salvation by inviting the children to make Jesus their "Forever Friend." That same invitation is extended to all of us. If you need a friend today, a friend who will never leave or forsake you, one who is a friend to "tax collectors and other sinners," then we encourage you to say "yes" to Jesus— for the first time or once again. He will be your Forever Friend.

[Jorge] Like Zacchaeus, my wife, Cheryl, experienced what it was like to be short on friends. Having spent her childhood in a small town in Kentucky, she moved as a teen with her family to Orlando, Florida, in the midst of the Disney boom. Cheryl, an only child, had attended a very small country school where everyone knew everyone. Orlando was a metropolitan city. Being a transplanted country girl, she spoke with a Kentucky accent and carried a mailbox lunch box to school. Her new citified classmates were ruthless in their teasing of her.

At the same time, Cheryl and her parents began attending a church that was exploding in growth. One night her youth pastor told her and the other youth group members that if they were lonely and hurting, Jesus was waiting to be their best friend and accept them just the way they were. That night Cheryl Lynn Montgomery, a lonely, displaced thirteen-year-old, asked Jesus to become her Friend—and he did. Like Zacchaeus, Cheryl's life changed after she met Jesus. Ever since he has been her Friend who has helped her make better judgments, brought out the best in her, and motivated her to live as Jesus lived.

Have you been trying to earn God's love? Are you in need of a Forever Friend who loves you just as you are? We invite you to become friends with Jesus or renew your friendship with him. We both have many friends for which we are very grateful—including each other—yet we can emphatically say there is no better friend than Jesus. He will forever call you by name and accept you just as you are.

2. God wants to give us forgiveness.

A second gift God gives us through his justifying grace is forgiveness. Zacchaeus certainly was in need of that.

The Greek word for tax collector is *telones*. These tax gatherers were usually Jews who collected taxes for Rome, and it was understood that they were to keep a "fraction" for themselves. There was really no way to prevent that "fraction" from growing to greater proportions, and, in fact, fraudulent extortion was encouraged. Yet Jewish law was clear that theft is a sin.

Zacchaeus was not just a *telones* or tax collector; he was an *architelones,* which was a chief tax collector. His kind was utterly despised and hated by fellow Jews. The bottom line for Zacchaeus was this: he had a lot to be forgiven of! He wasn't only a chief tax collector; he was a chief sinner. That's why Luke 19:6-7 tells us,

> *Zacchaeus quickly climbed down and took Jesus to his house in great excitement and joy. But the people were displeased. "He has gone to be the guest of a notorious sinner," they grumbled.*

Jesus made himself the guest at the home of a notorious sinner, and that is very good news for us.

For the past twenty years we both have prayed a simple yet profound prayer that has changed our lives and our church. It's just ten words: "Lord, send us the people nobody else wants or sees." And through the years, God has sent us women and men who did not feel wanted or even seen. From broken up-and-comers to lowly down-and-outers, God has brought to our church a mass and mess of humanity with their hurts, habits, and hang-ups. Our greatest joy as pastors has been getting this front-row seat to witness life change. Watching Jesus "wreck" a notorious sinner's life makes all the effort and heartache worthwhile.

Perhaps you're thinking, "I'm not a notorious sinner." We get it. We have spent far too much of our lives comparing ourselves and measuring ourselves to others. Here's how it works: We think about our lives, compare them to a notorious sinner like Zacchaeus or a murderer in the news, and we always come out looking good.

Yet remember the "goodness ladder." The standard for comparison is not with Zacchaeus but with Jesus. Think about Jesus' character and heart. One word we can use to describe Jesus is *love*. Paul wrote about love in 1 Corinthians 13, often called "the love chapter." The verses in that chapter beautifully describe love.

[Wes] A few years ago, I did something different in my journal. After reading 1 Corinthians 13, I replaced the word *love* with my name. I wondered, "What would it look like to put my name in those descriptions?" So I wrote . . .

Wes is patient.
Wes is kind.
Wes does not envy or boast and is not proud.
Wes is not self-seeking, not easily angered, and keeps no
*   record of wrongs.*
Wes does not delight in evil but rejoices in the truth.
Wes always protects, always trusts, always hopes,
*   always perseveres.*
Wes never fails.

As I struggled to write every line, the Holy Spirit began to reveal the truth of my soul and gently invited me to compare my character with God's character—not someone else's.

And the truth is that compared to the Lord's character, I am not patient or kind. I tend to envy, be boastful and proud. I am self-seeking and easily angered, and I really enjoy keeping records of wrongs. Compared to God's character, I delight in evil and do not rejoice in truth. Compared to God, I don't protect, trust, hope, or persevere. Compared to God, I don't measure up. You could even say I am a "notorious sinner."

Of course, none of us wants others to see who we really are, but God sees—and it is not a pretty picture. We once heard a pastor tell his congregation, "If you knew my sin, you would not let me preach to you." Then he followed that by saying, "If I knew your sin, I wouldn't preach to you, either!"

The Apostle Paul identifies himself in one of his letters as the "chief [of sinners]" (1 Timothy 1:15 KJV). He wasn't measuring himself against other people. He was examining his heart compared to the heart of Jesus. And Paul knew that the start of healing begins when we get honest. By ourselves, we can do nothing! There is power in powerlessness. One of the things we love about the recovery ministry at our church is that it begins with desperation. When it comes to sin's hold on our life, all of us are desperate for help that comes from outside ourselves.

Do you ever think about the worst sins you've committed? Or have you ever considered the good things God created you to do that you neglected? The good news of God's love through Jesus is that God's grace finds us—even now! What happens when we say "yes" to Jesus as our Savior is that our position before God changes. When we allow the gift of salvation to be applied to our sins and our lives, we become "justified." That means that when God looks at you and me, covered by the blood of Jesus that has the power to wash away sin, God does not see our sin. God looks at you and me "just-as-if-I-had" never sinned.

Because of this, the walls of hostility between God and us are supernaturally broken down. A change of heart occurs in us when we recognize our desperation and then trust that Jesus can do for us what we cannot do for ourselves. We become aware that we deserve punishment but receive mercy and forgiveness instead.

When John Newton was six years old, his mom died. After bouncing around between homes and boarding schools, he got a job as an apprentice sailor on a ship. John hated life, and life seemingly hated him. He wrote profane songs and poetry and mocked anyone who believed in God. He joined the navy but was dishonorably discharged after overstaying his leave. Limited in options, he got a job onboard a slave ship and was frequently in trouble.

One day John picked up a book called *The Imitation of Christ*, and a short time later, during a severe storm that washed another sailor overboard, John called out to God for mercy.[10] Years later he wrote a poem describing his life that we know as a familiar hymn:

> *Amazing grace, how sweet the sound*
> *that saved a wretch like me!*

I once was lost, but now am found;
was blind, but now I see.[11]

God loves us "even now," just as we are. This is God's soul-saving, justifying grace that is ours right now, today and every day—no matter who we are or what we've done. God does for us what we cannot do for ourselves, rescuing us by grace. None of us has to live life trying to "measure up." Grace means we don't have to "try harder" to earn God's love and forgiveness. We don't have to earn it. Grace is God's free gift through what Jesus Christ did on the cross, and there is no repayment schedule. All we have to do is welcome Jesus into our lives, just as Zacchaeus did.

Grace means we don't have to "try harder" to earn God's love and forgiveness.... Grace is God's free gift through what Jesus Christ did on the cross.

Zacchaeus was short on forgiveness. How about you? Hear this good news: "So now there is no condemnation for those who belong to Christ Jesus" (Romans 8:1). This is God's grandest offer of forgiveness, and all we have to do is say "yes." God's justifying, saving grace is available "even now."

3. God wants to give us a future.

Short on friends and short on forgiveness, Zacchaeus was also short on a future. He had no sense of purpose or destiny except to grow richer and become more and more lost in his loneliness, shame, and sense of meaninglessness. This one encounter with Jesus changed all of that. Having received the welcome of God as Jesus entered his home and his life, purpose exploded in Zacchaeus's empty soul:

> *Meanwhile, Zacchaeus stood before the Lord and said, "I will give half my wealth to the poor, Lord, and if I have cheated people on their taxes, I will give them back four times as much!"*
>
> (Luke 19:8)

Notice that Zacchaeus was not trying to climb the ladder anymore—including the ladder of trying to earn God's approval. A friendship with Jesus and the forgiveness Zacchaeus had longed for enabled a moral miracle to take place in his heart. Jesus' presence empowered him to set new standards of honesty and enjoy a new beginning. His sudden act of financial generosity came simply out of gratitude. He knew he had been loved much, and so he loved much, too. He pledged half of his wealth to the poor and then made another stunning announcement. Though the Mosaic law required him to pay back the money he had embezzled and add 20 percent (see Leviticus 6:5), Zacchaeus went well beyond that and quadrupled the restitution.

Dallas Willard, an exemplary follower of Jesus and a gifted author of many books on the spiritual life, wrote: "Grace is not opposed to effort, it is opposed to earning. Earning is an attitude. Effort is an action. Grace, you know, does not just have to do with forgiveness of sins alone."[12] Zacchaeus was not earning his salvation here. In response to amazing, unearned grace, he was putting his faith into action. The friendship and forgiveness that he had experienced through Jesus gave him a generous future.

Jesus had a front-row seat at watching a stingy, deceitful, self-centered man become an extravagant, joyful giver to others. Zacchaeus was a new man! He had a new purpose, a new destiny, and a new future because he met Jesus—who met Zacchaeus right where he was. Zacchaeus now had hope and a future.

[**Wes**] When she wasn't helping me shop for clothes for dates, my mom spent her career as an elementary school teacher. She took advantage of the opportunity to love children in a radical way, and her students responded to her ministry. One such student was a boy I'll call Randall. In kindergarten, he had such trouble that Mom spent an entire year focused on helping him change his heart and his behavior. Randall responded and won an award for most improved.

But one day in third grade, he returned to his old ways. He was disruptive to the point that the teacher—I'll call her Ms. Smith— had had enough and sent him back to visit with my mom for the day. Mom had him write a letter to his teacher. It went like this:

Dear Ms. Smith,

I want to tell you about the old and the new Randall. The old Randall is bad and doesn't listen to the teacher. The new Randall is nice and listens. He is kind and shares. The new Randall is very loving. Ms. Smith, I want to be the new Randall.

If you long to be the "new" you, if you are struggling with no hope or purpose in your life, accept Jesus' offer today. When Jesus claims us as a friend and cleanses us from sin, he also calls us to a life that matters into eternity. We accept God's offer to a future with joy-filled meaning simply by saying "yes."

It's Party Time!

Once we accept the friendship, forgiveness, and future that are ours through God's grace, it's time to celebrate! The party at Zacchaeus's house reached its crescendo as Jesus said: "Salvation has come to this home today, for this man has shown himself to be a true son of Abraham. For the Son of Man came to seek and save those who are lost" (Luke 19:9-10).

Zacchaeus was lost but now he was found. He was short on friends, short on forgiveness, and short on a future until Jesus came into his life. Salvation is more than "fire insurance"; salvation is a heart strangely warmed to the things of God. Salvation, said John Wesley, is not only about being delivered from sin but also about restoring our souls to their "original purity; a recovery of the divine nature; the renewal of our souls after the image of God."[13]

This was what happened to Zacchaeus. The very name *Zacchaeus* means "pure"[14] and "righteous."[15] He was starting to live up to this name. You see, Jesus transforms lives. Everyone is invited to receive God's justifying, soul-saving grace. When we both started planning our weddings, we had to decide whom to invite to stay within our limited budget. Not God! God invites everyone, "even now"!

The notion of God's love coming to us free of charge, no strings attached seems to go against every instinct of humanity. The Buddhist eightfold path, the Hindu doctrine of Karma, the Jewish covenant, and the Muslim code of law—each of these offers a way to earn approval and find forgiveness. Only Jesus dares to make God's love unconditional by coming down the ladder into our sin. When we realize this, understanding that we don't have to strive to win God's favor or earn God's grace, we truly have reason to celebrate.

[Jorge] When I think of celebrating salvation, I think of my mother's story. As I've mentioned, she was the one who "drug" me to church as a child. She always had a heart to know God, yet she struggled to understand God's grace. After I became a follower of Jesus and joined a vibrant local church, Mom would ask me questions about what I was learning and experiencing. Her thirst for God was insatiable. Yet her barrier to faith in the sufficiency of God's grace was a strongly held belief that good works are what connect us to God. I remember coming home from Bible studies, sitting on the end of her bed, and talking for hours about what I was learning about God's amazing grace. Mom would even come with me to church periodically. Tears would stream down her face during worship. She was on an all-out search for God who ironically was on an all-out search for her!

Two years passed, and Mom was still longing for her own relationship with God. By this time I had married my youth group sweetheart, and we were preparing to move to Kentucky where I would study to become a pastor. Several months before we moved, our church announced a women's retreat, and I bought my mother a ticket so that she could attend with my wife and mother-in-law.

On the Saturday morning of the retreat, I was in the little bungalow where Cheryl and I lived, praying for my mother to come to faith in Jesus. A friend had taught me to pray using the Psalms as a guide. When I knelt down on the floor with my Bible open to the Psalms and began praying for mom to experience God's "even now," justifying grace, the phone rang. It was my wife, Cheryl. "Jorge, your mom wants to talk to you," she said, and then she handed the phone to Mom. Mom said through tears, "Jorge, I just invited Jesus into my life." We wept together as my mother entered into the joy of her salvation.

After returning home, Mom told me what had happened at the retreat. On Friday, the retreat leader handed out a piece of construction paper to every woman with the instructions to tear out a shape that described her relationship with God right now. My mother made an arrow. In her small group, she held the arrow pointing up and said, "Right now in my relationship with God I am striving to know God." At the end of the retreat, after coming to faith in Jesus, my mother stood and held that same arrow, this time pointing down, and joyfully declared, "I had it wrong all those years. I thought it was about me striving to get to know God when, in reality, God sent Jesus down to this earth to get to know me. Jesus came to save me." That weekend, my mother's long journey to God was set on the path of justifying grace.

"Today is the day of salvation" (2 Corinthians 6:2). Will we say "yes"? When we do, we still have no idea of all that God has done to see us accept his offer. What we do know is that God sent Jesus from heaven to become a person like you and me. Jesus humbled himself so much so that the only time he was "lifted up" during his earthly ministry was to die on a cross for us. Jesus didn't get down on his knee to show us his love; he went down into a grave so we can find a friend, forgiveness, and a future. May our response be an enthusiastic, joy-filled "yes!"

CHAPTER 3

⟡

EVEN MORE
God's Character-Shaping Love

(Sanctifying Grace)

My response is to get down on my knees before the
Father, this magnificent Father who parcels out all
heaven and earth. I ask him to strengthen you by
his Spirit—not a brute strength but a glorious inner
strength—that Christ will live in you as you open the
door and invite him in. And I ask him that with both
feet planted firmly on love, you'll be able to take in
with all followers of Jesus the extravagant dimensions
of Christ's love. Reach out and experience the breadth!
Test its length! Plumb the depths! Rise to the heights!
Live full lives, full in the fullness of God.
(Ephesians 3:14-19 The Message)

[Wes] A number of years ago I experienced a very difficult time
in my life. My wife, Becky, and I were the proud parents of a three-
year-old son and had another boy on the way. Newly graduated

from seminary and commissioned as a pastor, I was sent to bring new life to a declining inner-city church. I was filled with vision and ready to prove myself as a "senior pastor" at the ripe old age of thirty-two.

Within days, however, I discovered the journey to "restart" the church was going to be difficult as I met with fierce opposition by the remaining members. Even though the average age was 82, the remnant of a once-proud church still had enough energy to protect their church from change. Yet, for me, the stress of leading this effort was nothing compared to what was going on at home.

One day when I was out of town for a meeting, Becky called me in a panic. "Honey," she said in a broken, frightened voice, "the police are here. A man followed Caleb and me home from the playground and broke in the house." She went on to describe how, as she arrived home with our toddler in tow, a man barged through the front door right after they entered the house. With her mother's instinct and strength, she was able to sweep up our toddler with one arm, knock over the assailant with the other, and flee to our neighbor's house for safety. Within a few weeks a suspect was caught, Becky identified him in a lineup, and he was arrested.

After that event, which included some nights hiding in a hotel while we waited for the arrest, we tried to return to normal. Ministry remained stressful as attendance dropped and I faced resistance from inside and outside the church over launching a Spanish-language service.

At the same time, we faced a new, horrifying challenge at home. During a routine check-up for our soon-to-be born son, Becky and I were informed that he had severe spina bifida and would not live after birth. We prayed for a miracle for little Daniel, and yet he died in our arms shortly after being delivered. We were heartbroken. On the day I had planned to buy a new cradle for my son, I bought him a casket instead.

Almost immediately after our son's burial, my grief gave way to furious anger. I began to argue with Becky to the point that we slept in separate rooms and avoided each other as much as possible. Our marriage was soon in serious trouble.

The person I was angry at the most was myself. Despite my best efforts, I could not save my son, protect my wife, or grow my church. I felt like a failure as a father, husband, and pastor. I believed I had let everyone down, including God. I tried to hide my rage and despair, especially on Sundays when it came time to deliver a sermon.

One Sunday as I stood up to preach, I noticed a familiar face in the sea of empty pews sprinkled with a couple dozen people. It was my old youth choir director, Bonnie Crandall, who came to encourage me. She had heard all that had happened and came to show her support. Three days later, I received a letter from Bonnie letting me know that in the years since I had talked with her, she had become a licensed pastoral counselor. What she wrote next changed my life. She saw through the public, "imposter-Wes" and noticed how badly I was hurting. She saw that while I was preaching about heaven, I was in my own private hell. She offered to help.

Just a few weeks later, I found refuge in Bonnie's office. She helped me see that I was unsuspectingly caught in a dangerous undertow of trying to live and navigate life on the "performance plan" we discussed in the last chapter. I lived and even ministered to others to prove my worth and earn the right to be accepted and loved.

I had become a follower of Jesus as a middle school student, and I had genuinely entrusted my life to him as my Savior. Yet the tragedies I faced revealed that I unknowingly viewed my salvation as a "90-days-same-as-cash" deal with God, where the grace that was free to begin with must be paid back through rigorous self-improvement. The difficulties in my life revealed that my attempts to "be like Jesus" were largely about my effort instead of my simple cooperation with God's grace.

It was in Bonnie's office each week over the next three years that I encountered the third "season" of grace—God's character-shaping, Holy Spirit empowered, sanctifying grace. I discovered it could transform an angry, anxious, grief-stricken, exhausted preacher of the good news of Jesus into a person who peacefully, authentically, and securely embraces the full life God intends for us.

With Bonnie's help, I began to claim my true identity as what she called a COGPOW: Child of God and Person of Worth. Bonnie's acrostic became a daily anchor for my soul and opened the door to God's character-shaping offer of grace. God used Bonnie to help me discover that God's grace not only provides a way to get to heaven *someday*; grace also starts a lifelong adventure of letting God love us so that God can move more of heaven into our hearts *now*. That's sanctification—the "even more" of God's grace.

Have you ever seen one of those commercials where they share a product, give you the price, and then say, "Wait...there's more"? One commercial we remember was the Ginsu knife. It could cut through everything, including tin cans and wood. It even came with a fifty-year warranty. And just as you thought the advertisement was ending, the announcer said, "But wait ... there's more!" and introduced a potato peeler that doubled as a chainsaw (or something like that). On and on the commercial went, with "even more" offered.

That's how grace is. Just as soon as you encounter grace, God says, "But wait, there's even more!" But God's not trying to get us to buy a Ginsu knife set or some other product. God wants to give us more grace. Yes, God wants to *save* us by grace, but God also wants to *transform* us by grace.

As believers in the Wesleyan tradition, we believe salvation is much more than "fire insurance" against eternal separation from God or a holy evacuation plan to escape earth. Salvation is when our souls are restored to wholeness and health so that we are free to love God, receive God's abundant love into our lives, and then freely love others. Loving God, self, and others is what it means to be sanctified.

Experiencing God's justifying grace is just the beginning of the Christian life. The day of your salvation is like your "spiritual birthday." After that, there is a whole new life to grow into and live. We regularly tell people, "If the only thing Jesus wanted to do was get you to heaven after your salvation, he'd kill you." To be a Christian is to be born again into a new life as a new person. When you say "yes" to Jesus as your Savior, the conversion from old to new, from darkness to light, from death to life is a miracle that happens in a moment or a season. But cooperating with God's grace so that you are transformed into the image of Christ takes a lifetime.

Just as little kids dream of the day they will be teenagers and teenagers dream of the day they will be adults, we have an invitation from God to "grow up" in grace. You see, God's sanctifying grace is God's "even more," character-shaping love.

Understanding Our Position and Condition in Christ

One of the pitfalls we get into when it comes to this ongoing pilgrimage of becoming more like Jesus is misunderstanding an important biblical concept. Throughout the New Testament there are statements that should fill us with boldness and confidence, such as Paul's word in Romans 8:1-2:

*So now there is no condemnation for those who belong to
Christ Jesus. And because you belong to him, the power of
the life-giving Spirit has freed you from the power of sin
that leads to death.*

What's not to like about this statement? It is a reality for every
Christian. Through Jesus' work on the cross and the tomb, we
have been freed from judgment and sin's insidious grip. Yet if we
are honest we have to acknowledge that we still have moments of
condemnation and still wrestle with sin.

Couple this with Paul's testimony just a chapter earlier in
Romans 7:18-20 as he described his struggle to do the right thing:

*And I know that nothing good lives in me, that is, in
my sinful nature. I want to do what is right, but I can't.
I want to do what is good, but I don't. I don't want to
do what is wrong, but I do it anyway. But if I do what I
don't want to do, I am not really the one doing wrong; it
is sin living in me that does it.*

So which is it? Are we freed from condemnation and sin's power
or are we sentenced to a life of fighting to do the right thing?

Could both realities be true? It seems to us that Paul sometimes
expounded on our "position in Christ." By this we mean that there
are statements such as "There is no condemnation for those who
are in Christ" that describe how God sees us. The redemptive work
of Jesus coupled with our trust in that work makes us positionally
freed and cleansed. This is our position in Christ.

But Paul also wrote about our "condition in Christ." This has
everything to do with how we as Christ-followers cooperate with
the Holy Spirit in the gift of Christian community to become more
and more like Christ. Paul's gut-wrenching honesty in Romans 7
captures this reality, too.

You see, as Christ-followers we are to practice what Jim Collins calls the "Genius of the AND" instead of the "Tyranny of the *OR*."[1] In other words, we must live in the tension between our position in Christ (what Christ says about us) and our condition in Christ (how we are in "real time" walking with Christ). Sanctification is the journey to close the gap between our position and our condition in Christ.

John Wesley called full or entire sanctification the "grand depositum" of the early Methodist movement.[2] This doctrine has been misunderstood to mean, "Don't smoke, drink, or chew— or go out with those who do." With that understanding, faith becomes a laundry list of do's and don'ts instead of a journey to joyful obedience. However, Wesley believed that a Christian can be made perfect in love. He believed that with this gift of God's "even more," sanctifying grace, the intention of the Christian's heart can be made complete or "perfect." Lost forever is the excuse, "Well, I'm just human," and in its place is an intimacy with God that is pervasive. This is the privilege of every follower of Jesus.

This is the type of change Paul longed for in his life. He yearned for "even more" grace. In Paul's letters we see that he was not satisfied with a fond memory of an experience of grace in the past; he was captivated by the mystery of God's grace more alive in him than ever each day. We are invited to experience grace in our lives this way, too. We need to position our lives so that we can experience and respond to grace, which brings us to the question of *how*.

How Can We Fully Experience and Respond to God's "Even More" Grace?

In Paul's letter to the church in Ephesus, he devoted the first chapters to bragging on God's grace expressed through Jesus dying on a cross for our sin and being raised to new life so that we can be in a relationship with God. Paul was in awe of grace. Having experienced grace, he felt compelled to respond. As the hymn says, "Love so amazing, so divine, demands my soul, my life, my all."[3] Our seminary professor Dr. Steve Harper said it this way: "Grace plus our response equals growth."[4]

Let's consider two ways we can experience and respond to God's sanctifying, "even more" grace.

1. We can love God and let God love us "even more."

[Wes] I grew up hanging around with youth groups. My parents worked a lot with teenagers in the church, and I had the joy of tagging along. I wanted to grow up to be like those "cool kids in youth group." I am grateful because the songs that they sang stayed with me. I remember hearing them sing the chorus from *Godspell*, which talked of three things to do more of "day by day"—seeing God clearly, loving God dearly, and following God nearly.[5]

This is a theme that Paul expressed in Ephesians 3:14-21 (*The Message*):

> My response is to get down on my knees before the
> Father, this magnificent Father who parcels out all
> heaven and earth. I ask him to strengthen you by
> his Spirit—not a brute strength but a glorious inner
> strength—that Christ will live in you as you open the
> door and invite him in. And I ask him that with both
> feet planted firmly on love, you'll be able to take in
> with all followers of Jesus the extravagant dimensions
> of Christ's love. Reach out and experience the breadth!
> Test its length! Plumb the depths! Rise to the heights!
> Live full lives, full in the fullness of God.
>
> God can do anything, you know—far more than you
> could ever imagine or guess or request in your wildest

dreams! He does it not by pushing us around but by
working within us, his Spirit deeply and gently within us.

Paul encouraged his friends to daily take in and experience the extravagant dimensions of Christ's love. To grow into the "fullness of God" means to seek every day to see, love, and follow God more and more. Loving God "even more" is our response to grace. What Paul was getting at is best understood in relational terms.

[**Wes**] I have been married to Becky for nearly twenty-three years. Before that, we dated for two and a half years, but I had my eye on her six months prior to that. That was our "even there" season. But on May 15, 1993, we had our "even now" moment when we got married. Our standing before God, the government, and our family and friends was officially husband and wife.

Now, what if we had walked out of that church and gone our separate ways? Would we still be married? Well, technically yes, until one of us got a phone call announcing that the other had died. But that was not my goal in marrying Becky. I made those vows, and through the years we've imperfectly struggled together so that our love for one another grows "even more." My prayer is that we will continue to grow in our love for one another "even more" until death us do part.

Our relationship with God is like that. God's "even there," prevenient grace is the dating season. God's "even now," justifying grace is the wedding day. That's a great day—something to celebrate and take pictures of and remember. But wait, "there's more!" Every day we are invited to know God more and grow in God's extravagant grace. The goal of grace is not to have a one-time experience when we accept Christ. God's "even more," sanctifying grace is the lifelong marriage of our relationship with God. The goal of grace is that we would love God more. As Paul says in another letter, "I want to know Christ…" (Philippians 3:10) more and more every day.

Sanctification Through Time with God

Knowing and loving God more takes time. Just as our relationships with people we love require meaningful time, so it is with our relationship with God. When those who are struggling in their spiritual lives come to us, we ask them this question: "When was the last time you spent time with God?" Usually it has been a long time since they spent time with God in prayer, Bible study, worship, or Christian community. Loving God takes time.

Both of us once served on a church staff with Richard "Dick" Wills, who used to teach that we needed to have an "up to date" faith. With great love he would say, "If you cannot tell me what God has been doing in your life for the last thirty days, I question whether you have a relationship with God." What God did in your life when you were at summer camp thirty years ago is great. That sermon that challenged you two years ago is wonderful. But how is your real-time walk with God? What is God teaching you? Where is God challenging you? How is God healing you? The disciple on the path of sanctifying grace can easily and quickly answer these questions.

[Jorge] A number of years ago I spent a week with a group of other pastors at the New Hope Christian Fellowship where Dr. Wayne Cordeiro is senior pastor. The week was designed for us to pick the brain of one of America's most effective pastors. It was supposed to be a "learn the tricks of the trade" experience. But God had a big surprise for me.

At age forty-two, with nearly twenty-five years logged as a Christ-follower, I honestly was still struggling with my daily devotional life. Spending consistent time with God had been a struggle for me since I came to faith in Christ at age eighteen. All of that changed during that one week.

On the first morning, Wayne invited my group to meet him for devotions at a coffee shop. When we got there, Wayne instructed us to jot down any insights that the Holy Spirit gave us as we read our Bibles. After forty minutes of reading and writing, Wayne led our group in sharing what we had learned. We read directly from whatever we wrote. It was a very cool experience.

Later that morning when we gathered at Wayne's office for our official time with him, he taught us how to have a quiet time using the SOAP method.[6] For the entire week, early each morning I met with Wayne and others to read from the Old and New Testaments and journal in response to one verse of Scripture. It was a transformational experience.

Several months later I presented a sermon series called "The University of the Holy Spirit" to introduce the people of our church to what I had learned from Dr. Cordeiro. Here are four simple steps to get enrolled in "The University of the Holy Spirit":

1. Set aside time every day to listen to the Holy Spirit (45 minutes to 1 hour).
2. Pray and ask the Holy Spirit to "highlight" some portion of the Scripture reading for that day. This will be the verse that "jumps off" the page at you.
3. Read both the Old and New Testament readings assigned for that day.
4. In a journal, write or type the following:
   - **S** - Scripture: This will be the one verse that the Holy Spirit "highlighted" for you as you read.
   - **O** - Observation: Jot down what you observe about this verse within its biblical context.
   - **A** - Application: Write down any "takeaways" or personal applications. Where does this verse touch your life?
   - **P** - Prayer: Close your time with a prayer, asking God to make this learning come alive in your life.

This simple process revolutionized my life and our church by helping us know and love God more and more through intentional time in God's Word and prayer.

According to research conducted by the American Bible Society, the number one predictor of spiritual health is daily Bible engagement. They report, "Reflection on Scripture is the most powerful spiritual practice to help people move forward in their love for God and others."[7] Our combined sixty-five-plus years of full-time ministry confirm this. The women and men we have observed who practice some kind of disciplined Bible reading coupled with prayer and journaling have soared in their faith. They have an "up to date" faith. They are growing in knowing and loving God "even more."

Jesus wants to save you from separation from God not only eternally but also here and now.

Sanctification Through Healing

Another way we can experience and respond to God's sanctifying, "even more" grace is through healing.

Jesus wants to save you from separation from God not only eternally but also here and now. It's God's "even more," sanctifying grace that makes this second part a reality. Many have described Jesus' ministry as threefold: preaching (declaring the Kingdom), teaching (explaining the Kingdom), and healing (demonstrating the Kingdom). Jesus' healing ministry was his ministry that healed broken bodies, calmed emotional distress, cast out demons, and even raised the dead.

We have had a growing and effective recovery ministry at our church for more than seventeen years. In that time, thousands of people have begun the journey of healing from their hurts, habits, and hang-ups through the Celebrate Recovery ministry. Begun by Pastor Rick Warren and John Baker at Saddleback Church twenty-five years ago, this ministry is a biblically based, Christ-centered, twelve-step program.[8]

Many churches are guilty of what we call "spiritual malpractice." This is offering Jesus the healer without providing the people, places, and processes where Jesus can do healing work. It's not good enough to simply preach or teach that God can heal us. We must have people, places, and processes for Jesus' healing ministry to be demonstrated. Sanctification includes the healing ministry of Jesus to help us find victory over our compulsive behaviors.

[Jorge] A southern preacher friend of mine once said, "You can't swing a dead cat in my family and not hit a drunk." I immediately said, "Amen," because that described my family, too. Addictions have been the "secret family business" for many of us. Sadly, my relatives of days gone by perfected addictions to alcohol, drugs, and other compulsive behaviors; and even sadder for me, I, too, became captivated by certain addictive behaviors. After becoming a follower of Jesus, the well-intentioned leaders of my church told me to pray more and read the Bible. Although those were good things to do, they did not heal the deep inner wounds of my life.

For many years I white-knuckled my recovery from alcohol addiction. Every once in a while I would "act out" and go on a drinking binge. My anger over my lack of recovery and healing would leak out, resulting in me raging at my wife and new son. It wasn't until I was in my first full-time ministry job as a seminary student that Wes's father, my pastor and boss, lovingly but firmly pointed me to a Christian counselor. Over the next three years, I spent many hours on his couch working through the principles of healing found in Scripture and the twelve steps. This was the beginning of my experience of Jesus' deliverance from the hell I was living in.

More than thirty years later, I still am working the steps of recovery and engaging in other healing ministry opportunities. Layer upon layer, God's "even more," sanctifying grace has peeled away those things in my life that keep me from being fully alive in Christ.

[Wes] I have followed Jorge's example of allowing God's grace to heal my broken places. As a grateful Christian in recovery from depression and anxiety, my life has been and continues to be changed by grace. The healing God has done in my life can be directly traced to the practice of renewing my mind with God's truth. Regular times of interacting with God's Word, God's people, and God's presence—as well as many hours with therapists and accountability groups—have transformed my broken life. Instead of exhausting personal effort, such as my former "performance plan," sanctifying grace invites me to simply cooperate with God's transforming power already at work in me.

Because we both are basketball fans, we have a basketball story to illustrate our role in the Holy Spirit's healing, transforming grace. In the 1990s, the Chicago Bulls were making their run of six National Basketball Association championships. One night superstar Michael Jordan scored sixty-nine points in one game! Reporters interviewed Jordan's teammate Stacey King, a backup center who had scored one point in the game. A joker by nature, he said that he and Michael Jordan had combined to score 70 points that night.[9]

Our involvement in sanctifying grace is an unequal partnership to be sure, but it is a partnership nonetheless. We must set aside time not only to be with God but also for God to heal our broken places. Transformation takes our cooperation.

2. We can love others "even more."

We both enjoy the show *Undercover Boss* where a rich and powerful CEO puts on a disguise and enters into the daily routine with regular employees to learn their stories. The best part is the ending when the boss sits down with each employee he or she has encountered. The boss reveals his or her identity and then usually offers praise and, sometimes, helpful correction to the employee. The boss then hands out gifts for college funds, a needed vacation, or training to go to the next level in the company. After each encounter, the employee is usually smiling from ear to ear and shedding tears of joy. Almost all of the employees are overcome with gratitude, saying something like, "Thank you! This is a dream come true; I don't know what to do to thank you!" Some hug the boss, others dance, and almost all go back to engage their work as never before.

That show reminds us a bit of the gospel. God put on a disguise by taking on the form of a man named Jesus and coming into our everyday, messy, ordinary lives. When Jesus reveals himself as our Savior, forgiving all our sins by his own blood, overcoming death so we never have to die, and positioning and presenting us to God the Father as perfect, what are we to do? Our "work" in response to this amazing grace is to love others even more. This is what Paul instructed Christ-followers in the first century to do:

> *In light of all this, here's what I want you to do. While I'm locked up here, a prisoner for the Master, I want you to get out there and walk—better yet, run!—on the road God called you to travel. I don't want any of you sitting around on your hands. I don't want anyone*

strolling off, down some path that goes nowhere. And
mark that you do this with humility and discipline—
not in fits and starts, but steadily, pouring yourselves
out for each other in acts of love, alert at noticing differ-
ences and quick at mending fences.

You were all called to travel on the same road and in
the same direction, so stay together, both outwardly and
inwardly. You have one Master, one faith, one baptism,
one God and Father of all, who rules over all, works
through all, and is present in all. Everything you are
and think and do is permeated with Oneness.
(Ephesians 4:1-6 The Message)

Paul was in chains and told his friends to start walking—or better yet, running—on the road God called them to travel. What is this road? It is to help others experience and know God's grace. We live in a world desperate to know God's love and grace. In fact, it is our charge as followers of Jesus and the body of Christ to help others.

One day as we were studying this exact passage from Ephesians in preparation for the weekend services at our church, we received an alert text from the high school where Wes's son is a student and Jorge's wife is a teacher. The message said that the school had been evacuated due to a bomb threat and that law enforcement was at the school.

As we prayed for safety for the faculty, students, staff, and first responders, we began to ponder *Who threatens to blow up a school?* followed by *What can transform that person?* Law enforcement and the judicial system could hold the person accountable, and they should. Counselors could help the individual make better choices, and they should. Educators could help with new opportunities, and they should. But it is the church—which consists of Christ-followers like you and me—who is charged with helping even the most violent persons know and experience God's grace; and we should!

To accomplish this divine mission, to complete this Christ-inspired charge, we must love even people who don't love us. This means we must love even people who are different than we are, people who threaten us, people who persecute us, people who are our enemies. It means that we must love and forgive and share grace with even "that person." We all have our lists (and each of us is probably on somebody's list, too). To experience and respond to grace means we must love others "even more."

At a conference we attended a couple of years ago, one of the amazing leaders was Horst Schulze, former president and COO of Ritz-Carlton Hotels. Horst's vision as a leader has "helped reshape concepts of customer service throughout the hospitality and service industries."[10] At the Summit, Horst shared his vision that enabled him to do this. His idea, which was rooted in Jesus' command to "Love your neighbor as yourself" (Matthew 22:39), was to make the Ritz Carlton hotel's motto "We are Ladies and Gentlemen serving Ladies and Gentlemen."[11] In other words, high regard is given to all involved.

As we listened, we thought our motto as followers of Jesus might be "We are COGPOWs serving COGPOWs"—children of God and persons of worth serving children of God and persons of worth. We are not "lording it" over one another, looking down on others from our lofty places of honor. No, the ground is level at the foot of the cross. There is only one Lord. We *all* are children of God and persons of worth, including the other people in our lives. This attitude change can lift our relational worlds to new levels.

Don't Stop

There is a famous anonymous quotation that says, "The two most important days in your life are the day you are born and the day you find out why." To love God and love others as we love ourselves is why you and I were created. Life is more than waiting to get to heaven. Full life is found in loving God, letting God love us, and loving others. This is how we are to respond to God's character-shaping, sanctifying, "even more" grace; and it is a process that continues until the day we meet Jesus face-to-face.

[Wes] My dad was a pastor for forty-four years. He preached hundreds of sermons and still would be preaching today if cancer had not taken his life at age sixty-two. On the day that Dad preached his last sermon, with his body and voice weak and frail, his message was "Don't Stop." He urged all followers of Jesus to press on because "the best is yet to be." "Don't stop" he said, "because God is calling you." I think that last sermon of my earthly father was enough to keep me going until I meet my heavenly Father.

That's what "even more" grace is about. Don't stop! Love God even more. Don't stop! Let God love you even more. Don't stop! Love others even more. Don't stop! There's even more!

CHAPTER 4

§

EVEN WHEN
God's Never-Ending Love
(Glorifying Grace)

*And I am convinced that nothing can ever separate us
from God's love. Neither death nor life, neither angels
nor demons, neither our fears for today nor our worries
about tomorrow—not even the powers of hell can
separate us from God's love. No power in the sky above
or in the earth below—indeed, nothing in all creation
will ever be able to separate us from the love of God
that is revealed in Christ Jesus our Lord.*

(Romans 8:38-39)

One morning a pastor friend of ours, Ed Horne, got a call to visit
a dying saint in his church. The woman had gathered with all of her
children that day and wanted him to serve them Communion and
pray with them as a family before she died. Ed gathered with the
family, they joined hands in a circle, and he prayed for God's grace
to be experienced as the matriarch of the family passed from this

life to the next. As he prayed, Ed felt his cell phone vibrate in his coat pocket. When he was finished praying, he walked outside and listened to the voicemail that the caller had left. It was a member of his own family notifying him that his first grandchild was almost ready to be born. Within a few hours, he received another phone call that the elderly saint had died.

Now get this mental image in your mind. At almost the very same moment Ed was saying "Goodbye! I'll see you later!" to one of his dying saints, he also was receiving notice that he would be saying, "Hello! Welcome to this world!" to his first grandchild. This is a picture of the life of grace from the cradle to the grave, from the womb to the tomb, from the first breath to the last.

Keith Getty and Stuart Townend wrote the words and music to the powerful song "In Christ Alone." In the first verse, they affirm that as followers of Jesus, our hope is built on the solid ground of Christ alone. From Jesus' birth to his death, the second verse proclaims Jesus' obedience to God's mission. Verse three explodes with a declaration of God's resurrection glory and victory over sin's curse and includes these powerful words:

> From life's first cry to final breath,
> *Jesus commands my destiny.*[1] *(emphasis added)*

This is the scope and scale of God's grace. Living in this grace, our life is secure. As the Scriptures say, "Nothing in all creation will ever be able to separate us from the love of God that is revealed in Christ Jesus our Lord" (Romans 8:39) and "perfect love expels all fear" (1 John 4:18). Living with no fear of death is a safe and secure place to live.

John Wesley, founder of the Methodist movement, was the fifteenth child and second surviving son of Susanna and Samuel Wesley. His father was the pastor of Epworth, a small village in

England. When John was age five, the Wesley home caught on fire in the night. All the children were removed safely from the house, but when they were counted, John was missing. A farmer from nearby spotted little John looking out of an upstairs window in the midst of the flames. Several neighbors climbed on each other's shoulders and pulled young John out to safety. Only moments after he was rescued, the entire house exploded in flames. For the rest of his life, John Wesley referred to himself "as a brand plucked from the burning," a Bible quotation from Zechariah 3:2 (paraphrased).

After graduation from Oxford, the Church of England sent John and his brother, Charles, as missionaries to the American colony of Georgia. While sailing to America, John saw a group of German Moravians who were unafraid of a great storm that nearly destroyed the ship. John himself was terrified by the storm and the thought of death. But those German Christians sang songs of faith without fear. Their personal faith and assurance impressed him greatly.[2]

John failed miserably as a missionary in Georgia. It was during this time he realized that he had never been truly converted. As he left Georgia for a return trip to England, he wrote in his journal:

> I went to America to convert the Indians; but O, who shall convert me? Who shall deliver me from this heart of unbelief? O, who will deliver me from the fear of death? I have a fair summer religion. I can talk well; nay, and believe myself, while no danger is near: But let death look me in the face, and my spirit is troubled. Nor can I say, "To die is gain."[3]

John was very much afraid to die at this point in his life.

When he returned to London, John had a providential meeting with Peter Bohler, a member of the group of German Moravians who had impressed him with their braveness during the storm at sea. Peter Bohler was a kind of spiritual director to Wesley, instructing him in how to experience a genuine conversion. And on May 24, 1738, John Wesley experienced an explosion of God's grace in his life. He made this notation in his journal:

> In the evening I went very unwillingly to a society in Aldersgate, where one was reading Luther's preface to the Epistle to the Romans. About a quarter before nine, while he was describing the change which God works in the heart though faith in Christ, I felt my heart strangely warmed. I felt I did trust in Christ, Christ alone for my salvation; and an assurance was given me that he had taken away my sins, even mine, and had saved me from the law of sin and death.[4]

That night God began a movement in John that spread to a small band of his friends and ultimately throughout England and the Americas. That night he not only received assurance of his salvation but also overcame the fear of death. This is the gift of God's "even when," glorifying grace. This is God's never-ending love for us that enables us to live and die well.

Dying Well

[Jorge] In my first year of college as I was preparing for ministry as a pastor, I heard a preacher speak in chapel about the transition of our lives from sanctifying grace to glorifying grace. He told the story of going to the hospital one day to visit two men from his church who were dying. One man was a seasoned follower of Jesus who had many years of walking with God. The other man was a recent convert whom Jesus had rescued from a life of drugs and crime.

When the pastor entered the room of the saintly man, his loving family surrounded him. The old man was near death, coming in and out of consciousness. But as he lay there knocking on heaven's door, he mumbled the great hymns of the faith and quoted Bible verses. He was dying well.

The young convert, who had not had much time for the Holy Spirit to gently and carefully transform his character by sanctifying grace, had a different kind of experience at death. Vile words spewed from his mouth as he fought death and transitioned from this life to the other.

God's "even there," prevenient grace wooed both men to Jesus. God's "even when," justifying grace saved both men. Shortly, God's "even there," glorifying grace would welcome both men into eternity. What was the difference between these two men? The saintly man had had time to experience and live in God's "even more," sanctifying grace while, sadly and tragically, the younger man had not. The beauty of God's grace is that upon death, *both* men entered into the presence of the One who loved them most and best. But as followers of Christ, we all want to die well.

John Wesley taught the early Methodists to live lives so that they could die "good deaths." A physician who treated several Methodists made this claim to Charles Wesley:

> *Most people die for fear of dying: but I never met with such people as yours. They are none of them afraid of death; but [are] calm, and patient, and resigned to the last.* [5]

John Wesley himself was a student of what was called "the art of dying." He and his people knew how to die well. So, how can we be like them? How can we die well? Let us suggest two simple yet profound ways.

1. We can die well when we
live confidently in Christ **now**.

Dying well is a process that begins on this side of the veil of death as we live fully in Christ. The Apostle Paul demonstrated this well.

Paul was an amazing man. Called by many "the thirteenth apostle," this man who had been an enemy of the church and had been responsible for the deaths of many Christians became—by God's prevenient, justifying, and sanctifying grace—a pillar of the church. In fact, he was God's primary instrument to bring the good news to non-Jews. It's not a stretch to say that if you are a Christ-follower today, then you can thank Paul when you get to heaven.

Paul was at the end of his life and ministry, imprisoned in Rome for his faith in Jesus, when he wrote to his spiritual son, Timothy, tender words of encouragement, admonition, and parting. At the end of what many scholars believe was his last letter, he wrote these affectionate words to Timothy:

> *As for me, my life has already been poured out as an offering to God. The time of my death is near. I have fought the good fight, I have finished the race, and I have remained faithful.*
>
> *(2 Timothy 4:6-7)*

Paul was not afraid of death. He stated it clearly: "The time of my death is near." Can we ask you—are *you* afraid of death? Are you "death averted"? Our culture glamorizes youth and beauty and denies the reality that the mortality rate still hovers right at 100 percent.

Hear this truth from Paul: the secret of dying well is living well! Paul lived well. His life had been poured out. He had fought the good fight and finished the race. He was faithful to God. He lived well.

Dying well is a process that begins on this side of the veil of death as we live fully in Christ.

Paul also wrote, "For to me, to live is Christ and to die is gain" (Philippians 1:21 NIV). These are the words John Wesley quoted in his journal on his way home from his miserable missionary experience in Georgia—except they were not words he could claim for himself. Rather, they conveyed the longing of his heart. They described what he had seen in those Moravian followers of Jesus but he himself lacked. The fear of death had robbed him of the confidence to live now.

Paul's confidence was secure because he knew that whether he lived or died, he belonged to Jesus. That gave him great confidence in living. Because he belonged to Jesus in this life, he believed that being with Jesus in the life to come would be even more glorious. That's living well. When our lives belong to Christ on this side of the veil of death, not even death scares us.

Christian Community

One significant way of living confidently in Christ now is to live in Christian community. It's not a stretch to say that if you abhor Christian community on earth, it's going to be a bummer for you in eternity. God lives in eternal community in the Trinity. The Father, Son, and Holy Spirit mysteriously live in community. Two stories help to illustrate this.

[Jorge] Linda (not her real name) was a friend I made at my first church appointment after seminary. We quickly became dear friends because we both graduated from the same college—though many years apart. You see, Linda was in her eighties and I was in my twenties when we became friends. She used to come to the church on weekdays, prop open the door to the Sunday school room across from our offices, and play hymns on the piano. The notes would drift across the offices, bringing the presence and peace of God.

Linda and I stayed in touch even after we both moved. One day I called her and asked what she, now in her nineties, had done that day. She answered, "Oh, I rode my three-wheeler up to the nursing home where the old people live and played hymns for them!" Linda was living well now so she could die well later. She knew the importance of Christian community.

Years later, when I was serving on staff at a large church, one of my assignments was overseeing the small-group ministry. One afternoon, a high-powered businessman came to the church and asked to see me. As he sat in my office with his eyes welling with tears, he told me that he had just come from the funeral of an executive from his company who had died. "Pastor," he said, "there were only two people at his funeral. Me and his ex-wife. No kids or grandkids. No friends or work colleagues." Then as he wiped away his tears he said, "And I'm afraid that's going to be me. I excel at work but I'm failing in my faith. I need to join one of those small groups that you always talk about. Can you help me?"

I was humbled and honored at his request, and within a few hours I had connected him with a small-group leader. Almost one year later, he stopped me in the foyer of church as he and his wife were going to worship with their small group. He had tears in his eyes again, but this time for a different reason. "Pastor Jorge, thank you for connecting me with this group," he said. "My life has been transformed. I know who will be at my funeral." With that we embraced, and he went off to worship with his beloved Christian community. Living confidently in Christ now was preparing my friend to die well.

Holy Living

Another way to live confidently in Christ now is to cultivate holy living. This requires intentional self-examination. Stephen Covey wrote that highly effective people "begin with the end in mind."[6] One of his suggested exercises is to think about what you want the most important people in life to say about you at your funeral. What do you want your spouse, roommate, children, friends, and coworkers to say about you? Or as the bumper sticker says, "Live so that your preacher doesn't have to lie about you at your funeral!" Another way of thinking about it is to consider what you want your obituary to say. Paul wrote his obituary this way: "I've run the good race and I've fought the good fight. I'm ready to die."

John Wesley suggested that ignoring death robs us of the opportunity to examine the condition of our souls and to attain peace with God. In his address titled "A Word to an Unhappy Woman," Wesley wrote:

> Do you never think about [death]? Why do you not? Are you never to die? Nay, it is appointed for all men to die. And what comes after? Only heaven or hell. Will the not thinking of death, put it farther off? No; not a day; not one hour.[7]

Contemplating the end of our earthly existence allows us time to examine our standing with God in a focused and honest way that leads to life change.

In his classic book *Revelation: Holy Living in an Unholy World*, Robert Mulholland explains that the Book of Revelation is not some coded puzzle to be solved or novel with clues to figure out.

He argues that many first-century followers of Jesus would have understood the images of this vision of John the apostle and that the real goal of the book was to help persecuted followers of Jesus gain strength to stay faithful to Jesus in spite of horrific persecution.[8] God's "New Jerusalem" citizens would indeed live within unholy "Fallen Babylon" and could remain faithful to Jesus. So it was an encouragement for followers of the Way to live holy in an unholy world.

Dr. Mulholland categorizes Revelation 2 and 3, where Jesus speaks to the seven churches in Asia Minor, as "the good, the bad and the ugly." Indeed, mixed into Jesus' words to these seven churches are words that encourage the good, challenge the bad, and correct the ugly living of these much-persecuted early followers of Jesus.

To the missionary outpost in Smyrna, Jesus offers comfort by acknowledging that he has seen the suffering and pain they have endured:

> *"Don't be afraid of what you are about to suffer. The devil will throw some of you into prison to test you. You will suffer for ten days. But if you remain faithful even when facing death, I will give you the crown of life."*
> *(Revelation 2:10*, emphasis added*)*

"Even when" they face death, Jesus promises to give them "the crown of life." Life wins out over death in the end.

To the fellowship of Christ-followers in Pergamum, Jesus' heavenly "location services" means that he sees what they are enduring to stay faithful to the gospel.

Jesus says to these beleaguered disciples:

> *"I know that you live in the city where Satan has his throne, yet you have remained loyal to me. You refused*

> to deny me even when *Antipas, my faithful witness,*
> *was martyred among you there in Satan's city."*
> *(Revelation 2:13,* emphasis added)

"Even when" one of their members is killed for his faith in Jesus, they remain faithful to Jesus and his mission in the world.

These first-century Christians had cultivated a way of holy living now so that they could boldly face death whenever it came. They, along with our Moravian sisters and brothers of Wesley's day, cultivated a life in grace that gave them supernatural confidence.

[**Wes**] I saw this supernatural confidence in my dad who showed me not only how to live in faith but also how to die in faith. I drove Dad to the Hospice House just hours before he died from cancer. In our final moments alone together, his last words to me were simply these: "Well, Wes, let's go get this done." Dying was not Dad's destination; life was! Life *is!* Dad viewed death as we view a ticket counter or security checkpoint at the airport. Death is something that is part of the journey, but it is not the destination. We are not the living traveling to the land of the dying; rather, we are traveling from the land of the dying to the land of the living. Death is just getting ready to "fly away"! Dad lived confidently in Christ all of his life so that at the end of his life he could die well.

2. We can die well when we know we will live completely in Christ *then.*

Basil was a retired insurance salesman turned evangelist who called every first-time guest who visited our church. We've done some math. On an average Sunday during those ten years, we would have had eight identified, first-time guests. Basil called them all. That's 416 conversations a year. Betty, his wife, baked muffins to be delivered to those guests. That means Basil also arranged for 416 muffin deliveries per year. But that's not all Basil did.

Basil greeted everyone before each of our three services near the entrance to our church. We've estimated that on any given Sunday, Basil greeted and shook hands (if not hugged) about 300 people a week or 15,600 a year. Now think about this. He made 416 phone calls, arranged for 416 muffin deliveries, and made 15,600 personal greetings each year for ten years! One day he told us, "This is the richest time in my walk with God that I have ever known."

The Sunday morning before Basil died, he was at his post greeting people before and after services. Age and disease had taken a toll on him. We tried to give him a chair to sit in, but he refused. Less than twenty-four hours later, Basil stepped from this life into the next. His service to God testified to the mantra, "If you ain't dead, you ain't done." Basil's confidence in Christ in this life gave way to his completeness in Christ in death.

As he stood confidently in death's doorway, the Apostle Paul made a shift in his letter to his spiritual son Timothy from temporal life to life eternal. He wrote:

> And now the prize awaits me—the crown of righteous-
> ness, which the Lord, the righteous Judge, will give me
> on the day of his return. And the prize is not just for me
> but for all who eagerly look forward to his appearing.
> (2 Timothy 4:8)

It's as if Paul was saying, "On the other side of the door, my son, is awaiting the prize of my life. It's the prize of being with God and seeing Jesus face to face again. The last time I saw him was when he met me on the Damascus Road. Then I was a hater of Jesus. That day, Jesus transformed my life. And now I will see him face to face again." Paul knew that heaven and eternity awaited him on the other side of death's veil. It was his reward.

Paul was not only confident in this life but also confident about the next life. He knew that through the thin veil of death awaited his completeness in Christ. His words to the Corinthians tell us why he was confident:

Then, when our dying bodies have been transformed into bodies that will never die, this Scripture will be fulfilled:

> *"Death is swallowed up in victory.*
> *O death, where is your victory?*
> *O death, where is your sting?"*

For sin is the sting that results in death, and the law gives sin its power. But thank God! He gives us victory over sin and death through our Lord Jesus Christ.

(1 Corinthians 15:54-57)

Paul was not "death averted." He lived with a courageous, deep-seated conviction that in Jesus' death, burial, and—most importantly—resurrection that death, hell, sin, and the grave had been defeated. Jesus' bold declaration "It is finished" resonated through Paul's soul in this life so that he lived assured of life eternal.

Now, please do not misunderstand us to say that if you live confidently in Christ before death, you are promised a "Hallmark moment" death with your family praying and singing hymns around you. That may happen. We have been with many as they passed from this life to the next, and it was indeed one of those tender moments. But sometimes death comes as a surprising, unwelcomed visitor that even may bring physical pain and relational heartache. A heart attack or car accident can quickly and tragically steal a life away. Whether death comes to you slowly or quickly, whether it comes late in life or way too early, the Bible teaches us that if you are a follower of Jesus, you do not need to fear death.

Think about the death of Dietrich Bonhoeffer, the Lutheran priest who was hung by the Nazis for trying to overthrow Hitler. A prison doctor who witnessed the final moments of this brave Christ-follower's life wrote this of Bonhoeffer's final moments in this life:

> Through the half-open door in one room of the huts I saw Pastor Bonhoeffer, before taking off his prison garb, kneeling on the floor praying fervently to his God. I was most deeply moved by the way this unusually lovable man prayed, so devout and so certain that God heard his prayer. At the place of execution he again said a short prayer and then climbed the steps to the gallows, brave and composed. His death ensued after a few seconds. In the almost fifty years that I worked as a doctor, I have hardly ever seen a man die so entirely submissive to the will of God.[9]

That's dying well, sisters and brothers!

[**Jorge**] Howard Olds, Wes's father, was my first mentor. As Wes said earlier, in his last sermon before he died, this faithful pastor told his flock, "Don't stop!" That Sunday afternoon after preaching at my own church, I called my spiritual father. His voice was weak and shaky. I asked him how he was doing, and he said he was tired. Then I told him how much I loved him and how grateful to God I was for his profound influence on my life. My last words to Howard were, "Bubba, you left it all on the field. All on the field." And he did. Howard lived well so that he could die well!

[**Wes**] My father's father, Papaw Olds, was orphaned at eleven years old. He had to drop out of school in the sixth grade and go to live on a neighbor's farm and work to earn his room and board. In his mid teens, he got a job laying rails for the railroad. He was quick tempered and didn't back down from a fight.

When he was sixteen, he started "courting" my grandma. She made it clear that if they were going to be together, he'd be going to church. One day the love of God reached him, and he said "Yes" to Jesus as his Savior. He got connected to that local church, which launched a lifetime of spiritual growth as he learned to abide in Christ. He saved and bought a farm where he raised his family. His reputation in his town was stellar, and he never stopped growing and maturing in Christ. He even discovered how to say "I love you" to us, something that he had to learn from Jesus.

Papaw devoted time every day to reading the Bible and applying it to his life. At our last big family Christmas get-together, we converted a physical therapy room into a dining room. After supper, my dad slipped Papaw his Bible and asked him to read the Christmas story to us one more time. He did. Then, like a preacher with one last message to deliver, he launched into a thirty-minute sermon affirming his faith, appreciating his life, and letting all of us know he was ready to move on. He said, "I don't know what heaven is like, but I intend to find out soon. Preachers are always telling me that Christ is coming again, but I don't have time to wait for his return."

The last time I went to visit him, I asked if there was anything that he needed or wanted from me. He said, "Yes. Would you please read the last part of the Book of Isaiah to me? I'm not sure I'll get to finish it again." I opened up his well-worn Bible and read for a long time—all the way to the end of Isaiah. Then we said goodbye, and I left.

On the day he died, he caught a vision of a door opening up. He told my Uncle Bill, "If you can get me to the door, I'll be all right." At first they thought he meant the door to his room. But soon it became clear he was seeing another door. "Get me to the door," he repeated, "and I'll be all right." I don't know what he was seeing in that moment suspended between this life and the next. I like to think he was hearing the voice of his very best friend, Jesus, the one who says in the Book of Revelation: "Look! I stand at the door and knock. If you hear my voice and open the door, I will come in, and we will share a meal together as friends" (3:20).

On that day, Papaw arrived at his destination. In that moment, he experienced God's glorifying grace. He had lived well, so he died well. And so can you. This is the gift of God's "even when," glorifying grace.

Epilogue
Grace Ain't Fair!

*"For the Kingdom of Heaven is like the landowner who
went out early one morning to hire workers for his
vineyard. He agreed to pay the normal daily wage and
sent them out to work.*

*"At nine o'clock in the morning he was passing through
the marketplace and saw some people standing around
doing nothing. So he hired them, telling them he would
pay them whatever was right at the end of the day. So
they went to work in the vineyard. At noon and again
at three o'clock he did the same thing.*

*"At five o'clock that afternoon he was in town again
and saw some more people standing around. He asked
them, 'Why haven't you been working today?'*

"They replied, 'Because no one hired us.'

*"The landowner told them, 'Then go out and join the
others in my vineyard.'*

*"That evening he told the foreman to call the workers
in and pay them, beginning with the last workers
first. When those hired at five o'clock were paid, each
received a full day's wage. When those hired first came
to get their pay, they assumed they would receive more.
But they, too, were paid a day's wage. When they
received their pay, they protested to the owner, 'Those
people worked only one hour, and yet you've paid them
just as much as you paid us who worked all day in the
scorching heat.'*

*"He answered one of them, 'Friend, I haven't been
unfair! Didn't you agree to work all day for the usual
wage? Take your money and go. I wanted to pay this
last worker the same as you. Is it against the law for
me to do what I want with my money? Should you be
jealous because I am kind to others?'*

*"So those who are last now will be first then, and those
who are first will be last."*

(Matthew 20:1-16)

Inside all of us is a gauge that measures fairness, and it seems
right. We want crime and punishment to match. It's fair. When we
pay for services, we want the right amount and the quality we paid
for. It's fair. When we work on a paper, put in the time, do the work
the professor asked for, we have a sense of the grade we deserve.
It's fair.

This parable of Jesus about the nature of God's kingdom destroys
our sense of fairness. It challenges our fairness gauge. In this story,
Jesus tells us about a benevolent landowner who hires day laborers
to work in his estate. Workers in Jesus' day worked from 6:00 a.m.
to 6:00 p.m. for a denarius—the fair wage of the day. So as expected,
the landowner hires men to work at 6:00 a.m., but then he returns

for more workers at 9:00 a.m., noon, 3:00 p.m., and, unbelievably, 5:00 p.m.—just one hour before quitting time.

To this point, the story seems fair. As the whistle blows, indicating the end of the workday, the landowner instructs the foreman to pay the workers beginning with the last hired and working back to those hired twelve hours earlier at 6:00 a.m. This does not seem wise, especially given that the landowner plans to pay those who were hired last the same amount as those who were hired first.

As those who were hired last are paid, those who were hired early are quivering with excitement. These men had thoughts of a huge cash windfall. Why? It's fair! But their sense of fairness was about to be challenged. The foreman calls those hired at 3:00 p.m., and just like those hired at 5:00 p.m., they receive a denarius.

Our hunch is that the fellows hired at 6:00 a.m. are still holding out hope for a bigger payday. Think about it, the guys who worked three hours are still getting a heck of a deal, but surely the owner is going to pay those who worked twelve hours more, right? It's fair! But no. All the way down the line of day laborers, the foreman pays each man the same wage, regardless of the amount of work he has done.

The all-day workers begin to grumble, "This ain't fair! We worked all day and received the same as the guys who worked one hour." Look at the landowner's response:

> He answered one of them, "Friend, I haven't been
> unfair! Didn't you agree to work all day for the usual
> wage? Take your money and go. I wanted to pay this
> last worker the same as you. Is it against the law for
> me to do what I want with my money? Should you be
> jealous because I am kind to others?"
>
> (Matthew 20:13-15)

The landowner challenges the workers' sense of fairness with his generosity. He has paid everyone a day's wage, and those who worked longer do not like it one bit.

Frankly, neither do we, because we like fairness. Left to ourselves, the world would be managed by the mantra *Don't do the crime if you can't do the time!* Why? Because life should be fair! Yet Jesus challenges our innate sense of fairness in this story about the kingdom of God. In these verses, we see three insights that can help us navigate the unfairness of grace.

1. God's grace challenges our sense of fairness.

In Jesus' parable, the owner of the vineyard was guilty of unfair labor practices. Let's be crystal clear about that. Yet isn't this the nature of grace? One commentator wrote of this story:

> Jesus is not laying down principles for resolving union-management disputes. On the contrary, "the principle in the world is that he who works the longest receives the most pay. That is just. But in the kingdom of God the principles of merit and ability may be set aside so that grace can prevail."[1]

Jesus is telling us something about the character of grace and the God who extends it to humanity.

You see, there is such a thing as one-twelfth of a denarius. It was a coin called a *pondion*. The workers hired at 5:00 p.m. deserved a pondion. They worked one-twelfth of the day. But the generous landowner paid them eleven-twelfths more. Here's the deal. There is such a thing as a one-twelfth of a denarius, but there is no such thing as one-twelfth of God's love. God's love is extravagant and unfair.

Jesus modeled this grace when he hung between two thieves. Remember how one of the thieves mocked Jesus while the other asked for grace:

> *Then he [the thief] said, "Jesus, remember me when you
> come into your Kingdom."*
>
> *And Jesus replied, "I assure you, today you will be with
> me in paradise."*
>
> *(Luke 23:42-43)*

Fairness does not allow for this kindness stuff, but grace does. Fairness says, "You did the deed. You pay the piper." Grace says, "Today, regardless of your deeds, if you ask you will enter into God's presence."

2. We can either rage or rejoice over grace.

In Jesus' story, those hired first raged. Those hired last rejoiced. The real question for us to consider is: *Which am I?*

You may know the story of the two sons Jesus tells in Luke 15. After a younger son returns home with his tail between his legs for wasting his father's fortune, the grateful, benevolent father does not reprimand the wayward boy but throws a homecoming party. It was the response of the older son that challenges those of us with an acute sense of fairness:

> *Meanwhile, the older son was in the fields working.
> When he returned home, he heard music and dancing
> in the house, and he asked one of the servants what was
> going on. "Your brother is back," he was told, "and your
> father has killed the fattened calf. We are celebrating
> because of his safe return."*
>
> *The older brother was angry and wouldn't go in. His
> father came out and begged him, but he replied, "All
> these years I've slaved for you and never once refused
> to do a single thing you told me to. And in all that time
> you never gave me even one young goat for a feast with*

my friends. Yet when this son of yours comes back after squandering your money on prostitutes, you celebrate by killing the fattened calf!"

His father said to him, "Look, dear son, you have always stayed by me, and everything I have is yours. We had to celebrate this happy day. For your brother was dead and has come back to life! He was lost, but now he is found!"

(Luke 15:25-32)

The older son raged instead of rejoiced. He embodied the saying "You can live in the Father's house and not have the Father's heart." Isn't it true that we who have been the recipients of the Father's love for a long period of time can forget about what it was like to be far from God? Isn't it true that when you have labored in the fields since sunrise, you have the awful possibility of raging at those who come to the field late?

In his book *In the Grip of Grace*, Max Lucado talks about this raging possibility in Christ-followers. In his winsome style, he challenges those of us in recovery from raging in response to grace with these words about Jeffrey Dahmer, the mass murder:

You know what disturbs me about Jeffrey Dahmer?

What disturbs me most are not his acts, though they are disgusting. Dahmer was convicted of seventeen murders. Eleven corpses found in his apartment. He cut off arms. He ate body parts. My thesaurus has 204 synonyms for *vile*, but each falls short of describing a man who kept skulls in his refrigerator and hoarded a human heart. He redefined the boundary for brutality. The Milwaukee monster dangled from the lowest rung of human conduct and then dropped. But that's not what troubles me most.

Can I tell you what disturbs me most about Jeffrey Dahmer? Not his trial, disturbing as it was, with all those pictures of him sitting serenely in court, face frozen, motionless. No sign of remorse, no hint of regret. Remember his steely eyes and impassive face? But I don't speak of him because of his trial. There is another reason.

Can I tell you what troubles me about Jeffrey Dahmer?

Not his punishment, though life without parole is hardly an exchange for his actions. How many years would satisfy justice? A lifetime in jail for every life he took? But that's another matter, and that's not what troubles me most about Jeffrey Dahmer? May I tell you what does?

His conversion.

Months before an inmate murdered him, Jeffrey Dahmer became a Christian. Said he repented. Was sorry for what he did. Profoundly sorry. Said he put his faith in Christ. Was baptized. Started life over. Began reading Christian books and attending chapel.

Sins washed. Soul cleansed. Past forgiven.

That troubles me. It shouldn't have, but it does. Grace for a cannibal?[2]

If we are honest with ourselves, we too have this unchecked tendency to rage against grace.

[Jorge] I came face-to-face with this demon in me when I was a seminary student. As I've alluded to previously, my family of origin has a high degree of dysfunction in it. I like to say that the Acevedos put the "fun" in dysfunction. I'm a first-generation Christ-follower who, by the mercy and grace of God, has seen every member of my family become a Christian. When my mother became a Christian in her late fifties, she immediately began to pray for my older brother, Hector, to be rescued from his life of addiction. Hector was a seventeen-year cocaine addict who lost every good job he ever had, three wives, and three children to his disease.

When I would call home, my mother would confess to me her concern and, most importantly, her prayers for my brother. He was the focus of her prayers. And on the inside, I battled. I would think to myself as I listened to Mom on the phone, *Hey, wait, Mom. I'm struggling, too. Cheryl and I have abandoned it all for the sake of the call. We moved to the middle of nowhere. We're living on poverty-level wages, eating macaroni and cheese with a hot dog cut up in it if we are lucky. We've got a baby who needs diapers. I'm sleep-deprived from school, work, and ministry. What about us? What about our prayers?*

I was raging against grace! Because the reality was, I was in the Father's house. I just didn't have my Father's heart. God's heart is much like my Mom's heart. God loves us equally, but he also loves us uniquely. On my best days, I knew Mom loved us the same, but because Hector was living far from God, he got the best of Mom's prayers.

One of our favorite authors is Brennan Manning. Brennan was an on-again, off-again alcoholic, yet he had an experience of God's grace that was undeniable. Near the end of his life, Brennan wrote:

> My life is a witness to vulgar grace—a grace that amazes as it offends. A grace that pays the eager beaver who works all day long the same wages as the grinning drunk who shows up at ten till five. A grace that hikes up the robe and runs breakneck toward the prodigal reeking of sin and wraps him up and decides to throw a party no *ifs, ands,* or *buts.* A grace that raises bloodshot eyes to a dying thief's request—"Please, remember me"—and assures him, "You

bet!" A grace that is the pleasure of the Father, fleshed out in the carpenter Messiah, Jesus the Christ, who left His Father's side not for heaven's sake but for our sakes, yours and mine. This vulgar grace is indiscriminate compassion. It works without asking anything of us. It's not cheap. It's free, and as such will always be a banana peel for the orthodox foot and a fairy tale for the grown-up sensibility. Grace is sufficient even though we huff and puff with all our might to try to find something or someone it cannot cover. Grace is enough. He is enough. Jesus is enough.[3]

Brennan rejoiced over grace! We really get to choose friends. Will we rage or rejoice over grace?

3. God invites us to join his outrageous, extravagant, generous church.

Most sermons on Jesus' parable about the landowner and the workers focus on God being benevolent and gracious. Yet Jesus begins this parable with those common words, "For the Kingdom of Heaven is like…" (Matthew 20:1). The Kingdom parables of Jesus—of which this is one—are about God's desire to bring the realities of heaven to earth using the people of God, the church. They are not simply stories about the nature and character of God; they also are about the nature, character, and calling of followers of Jesus. We who are citizens of God's kingdom are to be like the generous landowner. We are called to extend God's unconditional love to a world that is lost, broken, and hurting.

The church is getting a black eye in our day, particularly in North America. And frankly, we deserve it. Statisticians tell us that between 80 to 85 percent of the churches in North America are maintaining or declining.[4] It's not looking pretty for the North American church. Yet, we still believe that, as Bill Hybels writes, "the local church is the hope of world,"[5] because the church is the primary instrument charged with extending the grace of God to the world.

Our church is filled with people who have been transformed by God's grace. At a recent celebration service, we invited people whose lives have been transformed by Jesus through the ministries of our church to hold up placards. On the front was what their lives were like before they knew Jesus, and on the back was written what their lives are like now. Many other churches have done similar "posterboard testimonies."

Erick (not his real name) spent eleven years in prison. After being in and out of prison and rehab, he landed at our church and found Jesus, a God-honoring wife, and a fellowship of drunks and addicts who have been instruments of God's grace. When Erick held up his sign, it read "Guilty" with his prison number underneath it. When he flipped it over, it read "Not Guilty" with "Romans 3:23" beneath. Our church flipped out! Erick is a witness of God's unfair grace.

[Jorge] A few years ago I received a phone call from a friend in another city who met a person at a social gathering who had been touched by the kindness of God through our church. This young man had been in prison for years, has struggled with addictions, and now is a Christ-follower. He told my friend that he was radically loved and accepted by the people of our church. He told her about the kind words of encouragement he received here. He said we were a "hobo church." Those words were sweet to my ears! Every church should be a "hobo church"—a church where all are welcome.

Friend, grace ain't fair! Yet the God of the universe—Father, Son and Holy Spirit—so graciously, generously, and quite unfairly extends grace to us. May you live from the cradle to the grave, from the womb to the tomb, from your first breath to your last in God's grace.

Notes

Foreword

1. A Letter from Evelyn Underhill to Archbishop Lang of Canterbury," 1930, http://kg.vkk.nl/english/organizations/lcc.gb/lcis/scriptures/liberal /underhill/letters/archbishoplang.html.

Introduction

1. Francis Chan, *Crazy Love: Overwhelmed by a Relentless God* (Colorado Springs, CO: David C. Cook, 2008).
2. "Your Grace Finds Me," Matt Redman and Jonas Myrin, writers; © 2013 Thankyou Music (admin. worldwide at EMICMGPublishing.com, excluding Europe, which is admin. by Kingswaysongs) (PRS) / sixsteps Music / worshiptogether.com Songs / Said And Done Music (ASCAP) / Shout! Music Publishing (Admin. At CaptiolCMGPublishing.com)

Chapter 1

1. Andy Stanley, Leadership Essentials Podcast, *Trust vs. Suspicion: How to Create and Maintain a Culture of Trust in Your Organization,* http://store .northpoint.org/trust-vs-suspicion.html.
2. Oswald Chambers, *My Utmost for His Highest*, "The Missionary's Master and Teacher" (Grand Rapids, Michigan: Discovery House Publishers, 1992), September 22 (no page number).
3. "Ain't No Mountain High Enough," Nickolas Ashford and Valerie Simpson, Tamla Motown, 1966.

Chapter 2

1. Sam Shoemaker (republished by Carl "Tuchy" Palmieri), *Children of the Second Birth: What We Used to Be Like, What Happened, and What We Are Like Now* (BookSurge Publishing: April 16, 2009), 25.

2. *The Methodist Hymnal* (Nashville: The United Methodist Publishing House, 1968), 828.

3. Bill Hybels, "Show Me the Way," https://vimeo.com/81679479. Willow Creek Community Church, www.willowcreek.com /ProdInfo.asp?invtid=PR00694.

4. Mother Teresa of Calcutta, "The Family She Founded: Statistics 2015," http://www.motherteresa.org/07_family/family00.html.

5. N. T. Wright, *Simply Christian: Why Christianity Makes Sense* (New York, NY: HarperCollins Books, 2006), xi.

6. *Charis*, www.biblestudytools.com/lexicons/greek/nas/charis.html.

7. David Brooks, "Startling Adult Friendships," *The New York Times*, September 18, 2014, http://www.nytimes.com/2014/09/19/opinion /david-brooks-there-are-social-and-political-benefits-to-having-friends .html?_r=0, accessed July 8, 2016.

8. Tommy Walker, "He Knows My Name," www.tommywalker.net /behind-the-songs/2014/1/23/he-knows-my-name.

9. Joseph M. Scriven, "What a Friend We Have in Jesus," *The United Methodist Hymnal* (Nashville: The United Methodist Publishing House, 1989), 526.

10. Chris Armstrong, "The Amazingly Graced Life of John Newton," Christian History Institute, www.christianhistoryinstitute.org/magazine/article /amazingly-graced-john-newton/, accessed August 31, 2016.

11. John Newton, 1779, "Amazing Grace," *The United Methodist Hymnal*, 378.

12. Dallas Willard, *The Great Omission: Reclaiming Jesus's Essential Teachings on Discipleship* (New York, NY: HarperCollins Books, 2006), 61.

13. John Wesley, "*An Farther Appeal to Men of Reason and Religion*," in *The Works of John Wesley: Vol. VIII* (Grand Rapids, Michigan: Baker Book House), 47.

14. "Zacchaeus," www.biblestudytools.com/dictionary/zacchaeus/.

15. Warren W. Wiersbe. *The Wiersbe Bible Commentary: New Testament*. (Colorado Springs, CO: David C. Cook, 2007), 202.

Chapter 3

1. Jim Collins, *Built to Last: Successful Habits of Visionary Companies* (New York: Harper Collins, 1997), 10.

2. John Wesley, "Letters to Robert C. Brackenbury, Esq., Bristol, September 15, 1790," in *The Works of John Wesley*: Vol. XIII (Grand Rapids, Michigan: Baker Book House), 9.

3. Isaac Watts, "When I Survey the Wondrous Cross," *The United Methodist Hymnal*, 298.

4. Steve Harper, *The Way to Heaven: The Gospel According to John Wesley* (Grand Rapids, Michigan: Zondervan, 1983), 76.

5.   "Day by Day," lyrics by Stephen Schwartz, from Godspell (New York): Valando Music Inc.: New Cadenza Music Corporation, (1971) New York, N.Y.: exclusive distributor Valando Music Inc ©1971 1 score (48 pages): illustrations, portrait; 28 cm; © Copyright 1971 by Valando Music Inc. and New Cadenza Music Corporation.
6.   Wayne Cordeiro, *The Divine Mentor: Growing Your Faith as You Sit at the Feet of the Savior* (Bethany House, 2008) for instructions on the SOAP method.
7.   "Engaging Scripture is the #1 Predictor of Spiritual Health and Growth," American Bible Society, http://www.americanbible.org/uploads/content /engaging-scripture-is-the-1-predictor-of-spiritual-health-and-growth.pdf, accessed August 31, 2016.
8.   Celebrate Recovery® ministry, see www.celebraterecovery.com, accessed November 23, 2016.
9.   Kent McDill, *100 Things Bulls Fans Should Know & Do Before They Die* (Chicago, Illinois: Triumph Books, 2012), 149.
10. Horst Schulze, Get Global, http://getglobalexpo.com/speakers /horst-schulze/, accessed August 31, 2016.
11. Horst Schulze, "Creating World Class Service," 2015 Willow Creek Leadership Summit address. http://www.followthegls.com /leadership-lessons/gls15-horst-schulze-creating-world-class-service-2/, accessed October 24, 2016.

Chapter 4

1.   "In Christ Alone," words and music by Keith Getty and Stuart Townend, Copyright © 2001 Kingsway Thankyou Music (Adm. by CapitolCMGPublishing.com excl. UK & Europe, adm. by Integrity Music, part of the David C. Cook family, songs@integritymusic.com).
2.   John Wesley, *The Journal of John Wesley, January 23, 1736,* in *The Works of John Wesley,* Vol. I (Grand Rapids, Michigan: Baker Book House), 21.
3.   Ibid., 74.
4.   Ibid., 103.
5.   *The Journal of Charles Wesley,* April 3–September 22, 1741. http://wesley .nnu.edu/charles-wesley/the-journal-of-charles-wesley-1707-1788 /the-journal-of-charles-wesley-april-3-september-22-1741/. (The Wesley Center Online web site is a collection of historical and scholarly resources about the Wesleyan Tradition, theology, Christianity, and the Nazarene church. Copyright © 1993-2011. Wesley Center for Applied Theology, c/o Northwest Nazarene University. All Rights Reserved.) Accessed October 25, 2016.
6.   Stephen R. Covey, *The 7 Habits of Highly Effective People: Powerful Lessons in Personal Change* (New York, NY: Simon Schuster, 1989), 95.

7.   John Wesley, "A Word to an Unhappy Woman," in *The Works of John Wesley: Vol. VI* (New York: Emory and Waugh, 1831), 357.

8.   M. Robert Mulholland, Jr., *Revelation: Holy Living in an Unholy World* (Grand Rapids, Michigan: Zondervan Publishing House, 1990), 40.

9.   Eberhard Bethge, *Dietrich Bonhoeffer: A Biography* (Minneapolis: Fortress Press, 2000), 927-928.

Epilogue

1.   Frank E. Gaebelein, *The Expositor's Bible Commentary: Vol. 8: Matthew, Mark, Luke, with the New International Version of the Bible* (Grand Rapids, Michigan: Zondervan Publishing House, 1984), 428.

2.   Max Lucado, *In the Grip of Grace: Your Father Always Caught You. He Still Does* (Nashville, TN: Thomas Nelson Publishing, 1996), 31-32.

3.   Brennan Manning and John Blase, *All Is Grace: A Ragamuffin Memoir* (Colorado Springs, CO: David C. Cook Publishing, 2001), 193-194.

4.   "The State of the American Church: Plateaued or Declining," The Malphurs Group, www.malphursgroup.com/state-of-the-american-church -plateaued-declining/, accessed August 31, 2016.

5.   Bill Hybels, *Courageous Leadership: Field-Tested Strategy for the 360° Leader* (Grand Rapids, Michigan: Zondervan, 2009), 27.